THE CHRISTIAN COLLEGE
IN THE TWENTIETH CENTURY

Books by Bernard Ramm

VARIETIES OF CHRISTIAN APOLOGETICS
PROTESTANT BIBLICAL INTERPRETATION
PROTESTANT CHRISTIAN EVIDENCES
THE CHRISTIAN VIEW OF SCIENCE AND SCRIPTURE
THE PATTERN OF RELIGIOUS AUTHORITY
THE WITNESS OF THE SPIRIT
SPECIAL REVELATION AND THE WORD OF GOD

BERNARD RAMM

Professor of Systematic Theology and Christian Apologetics
California Baptist Theological Seminary

The Christian College
in the Twentieth Century

William B. Eerdmans Publishing Company
Grand Rapids, Michigan

The five lectures here collected were originally given as
THE CLARENCE EDWARD MACARTNEY LECTURES, 1961-1962
WHITWORTH COLLEGE, SPOKANE, WASHINGTON

Dedicated to

William Richardson White
Chancellor, Baylor University

PREFACE

In reading the literature on Christian higher education I came to the conclusion that only an encyclopedia could do justice to all the facets of the problem. I have turned away from any attempt to read ten books and synthesize then into an eleventh, finding a historical-biographical approach much more rewarding.

I am in general agreement with the theses of the men discussed in these lectures. I have gravitated towards those elements in their thoughts which I found congenial to mine. This means that the manner of communication in these lectures is indirect. I am speaking my mind through these five men. There is also progress in the lectures. The first two lectures lay the foundation for a higher Christian education and the last three wrestle with the modern problems. For the convenience of the reader I have appended a summary statement at the close of the lectures.

My own bibliographical tools are cited in the footnotes and in the select bibliography at the end of the book. Special mention should be given to the Autumn, 1961, issue of *Encounter*. The essay by Quirinus Breen on "The Church the Mother of Learning" is an excellent survey of Christian higher education and forms a supplement to my own approach in these lectures. In this same issue Parker Rossmann gives us "A Survey of Some Recent Literature on Christian Higher Education." For those who wish to read further there are bibliographies in Elton Trueblood, *The Idea of a College*; Alexander Miller, *Faith and Learning*; H. P. Van Dusen, *God in Education*; and (in the notes of) J. P. Gruenigen, editor, *Toward a Christian Philosophy of Higher Education*.

I extend my thanks to the President of Whitworth College, Dr. Frank Warren, and to the trustees for inviting me to give

7

these lectures. Special thanks are to be extended to Howard A. Redmond with whom rested the burden of particulars. Thanks are also to be given to David Logue for bibliographical help.

BERNARD RAMM

Seminary Knolls
Covina, California

CONTENTS

Lecture I

AURELIUS AUGUSTINE (354-430):
RHETORIC RECLAIMED

I. Introduction

Our task in these lectures is to review the basic issues in Christian higher education by means of a historical survey. From this survey we expect to gain wisdom for the task of Christian higher education in the twentieth century.

The university system of our civilized countries stems directly from the educational task of the Christian Church. Universities as we know them emerged from the cathedral and monastic schools of the medieval period. Thus from the very beginning of higher education we find the Christian Church deeply involved. The fundamental reason for this is that the Christian Church from its very inception was pledged to education. The Great Commission itself (Matt. 28:19-20) makes it clear that the evangelistic and missionary work of the Christian Church calls for an educational activity of the Church.[1] The educational activity prescribed in the Great Commission is seen perfectly exemplified in Paul. He instructed his pagan listeners in the Christian faith and, after winning them to Christ, led them deeper into the truths of Jesus Christ. The writer to the Hebrews uses the educational vocabulary of his times to exhort his readers on to Christian maturity.[2]

---

1. The verb *mathēteuō* means "to make into disciples." The word "disciple" is derived from the Latin *discere*, "to teach," and hence means the one taught, the learner, the pupil. The second verb, *didaskō*, is the common Greek word meaning "to teach."
2. Cf. William Barclay, *The Letter to the Hebrews*, pp. 47-50.

11

Two other forces pressed the Christian Church into educational work: the apostles needed to be replaced by other leaders, and the fast-growing Church needed more and more Christian ministers. In his second missionary journey Paul adopted Timothy as his understudy and began a form of apprentice education for the Christian ministry. Later in his writings Paul instructs Timothy to instruct in the Christian faith other men who in turn can instruct their successors (II Tim. 2:1-2). Here is a span of four generations of Christian ministers whose education was through apprenticeship. Eventually the apprenticeship method grew into the bishop's school, the catechetical school, the monastic school, the cathedral school, and then the university.

The university arose to meet a need for the Church and the state. Both required scholars and professional men.[3] The common need found its answer in the university. The word "university" meant a corporation. The students organized themselves into a "university" to protect their rights in the cities of their sojourn. Later the faculty also "organized" and out of the faculty and student organizations was born the medieval university. It is hardly stretching the truth to say that the first universities grew out of a student "co-op"! Eventually these organizations developed into the full-grown school with its faculties of law, medicine, literature, science, and theology.

It is now necessary to leap across space and time to Christian higher education in America. One writer estimates that there are 553,813 students in Christian institutions of higher learning.[4] These institutions include both Roman Catholic and Protestant schools and they range from the Bible Institute, which requires

3. It must not be imagined that these medieval universities were theological seminaries for the ordinary priest. The thorough education of the Roman Catholic priest was a development from the Reformation. For a study of schools, curricula, texts, student life, etc., in the Middle Ages, see L. J. Daly, *The Medieval University, 1200-1400.*

4. Earl J. McGrath, "Let the Church College Be Itself," *The Christian Century,* LXXVIII (Dec. 6, 1961), 1459.

a high-school diploma and teaches a handful of liberal arts courses, to the denominational universities. Out of this range of institutions, we focus attention upon the Christian college as such. We are not concerned with the large university which was founded a century or more ago by some church or group of Christian educators but which is today thoroughly secular except for a bishop or clergyman on its board. Nor are we concerned with the Bible college, an institution which is half Bible Institute and half liberal arts college. We are concerned with the liberal arts college which attempts to give a liberal arts education in a Christian environment and from a Christian perspective. Our task is to investigate such an adventure within the social and educational situation of the twentieth century. To do this, we shall pass in review the educational theories of five important men, and use them as our foil. We begin our investigation with Aurelius Augustine, the greatest Christian educator of the ancient Church.

II. The Importance of Augustine

There is good reason to start our investigation with Augustine, who was bishop of Hippo in North Africa. The greatness of this man has been recited too many times for us to do it again. Suffice it to say that his thought helped to lay most of the important stones in the foundation of Western culture. There was hardly an area of thought in the culture of the medieval period which he did not influence little or much. But Augustine's impact was not exhausted in the Middle Ages. Anyone conversant with contemporary literature in theology or philosophy or history knows that Augustine is still a man to be reckoned with.

Augustine was trained as a rhetorician. Training in rhetoric was the highest form of education among the Romans and the closest thing in the ancient world to a university education. Not only did Augustine go to a school for rhetoricians, but he learned his subjects virtually without effort. In his *Confessions* he attributes this facility for effortless learning to God and owns it as a divine gift.[5] His first employment was that of a teacher of rhetoric in Tagaste and then, in Rome, and again in Milan. It was while he was professor of rhetoric in Milan that he was dramatically converted to the Christian faith.

Augustine was a born genius. Not only did he learn without effort and without tutorial help, but he was also the superior of his class.[6] In his nineteenth year he was inflamed with a love for philosophy when he read Cicero's *Hortensius*. His own religio-philosophical journey took him to paganism, to Manichaeism, to Platonism, to Neo-Platonism, and then to Christianity. Augustine thoroughly learned the classical way of life, its culture, its religion, its philosophy, and its literature.[7]

A man of great learning, Augustine reflected deeply upon the theory of learning itself. He approached this problem psychologically, philosophically, and theologically. Psychologically, he taught that all learning is through symbols; philosophically, he taught that all learning is through illumination; and theologically, he taught that all learning is through Christ, the inner Teacher. His basic works in this area are his *Confessions*, *The Teacher*, and *On Christian Doctrine*.

For our purposes the most important book is *On Christian Doctrine*. It sanctioned for the Church the basic curriculum of ancient rhetorical education and helped to pave the way for its acceptance in the medieval universities. It is a text which has been read through the centuries perhaps by more students than any other text in the history of higher education. It was the first book from the writings of the Church Fathers cast into printed form.[8]

---

5. *Confessions*, IV, 16, 30.

6. *Ibid.*, I, 17, 27. This compares with Paul's statement in Gal. 1:14.

7. Augustine's extensive knowledge of Cicero (as well as the Roman culture of his time) is reflected in the review of a Mainz doctoral dissertation: Eberhard Peusch, "Cicero und die Civitas Dei," in *Theologische Literaturzeitung*, LXXXVI (Nov. 1961), 861-864.

8. Cf. *The Writings of Saint Augustine*, IV, 7 (in the series *The Fathers of the Church*).

III. AUGUSTINE'S OPINIONS ON HIGHER CHRISTIAN EDUCATION

When the Christian Church emerged in Roman civilization, it created its own schools.[9] Augustine had a school in connection with his work in Hippo. V. J. Bourke is bold enough to write that "the monastery of Hippo was much more than a quiet home for self-effacing men. It was really one of the first theological seminaries."[10] Augustine's "graduates" were in great demand by the ancient African Church.

Let us suppose that Augustine had purposed to found a Christian college rather than a theological seminary; and in honor of his own educational home let us name his school The Carthage Christian College.

(1) *The Carthage Christian College must build its curriculum around the seven liberal arts.*

Augustine's basic educational theory is expressed in his book, *On Christian Doctrine*.[11] A number of commentators on this work miss its entire point because they fail to grasp the significance of its introduction. There were men in the ancient Church (as there are in the modern) who maintained that all so-called learning could be dispensed with because the meaning of the Scriptures could be grasped without it. Augustine wrote his work to rebut such a position.

Augustine makes short work of this idea. *First,* such an idea is contrary to the experience of men. No other kind of knowledge is acquired in this mystical way, and there is no reason to

9. Cf. "Schools," in *Dictionary of Christian Antiquity*, II, 1846-1858. C. H. Haskins, in his little work, *The Rise of the Universities,* notes that the university in our modern sense did not exist in the ancient world. Those interested in education in the ancient Greek and Latin civilizations may begin with William Barclay's *Educational Ideals in the Ancient World,* and follow through with his excellent bibliography.

10. *St. Augustine's Quest for Wisdom,* p. 26.

11. *On Christian Doctrine,* Preface, 5. Hereafter this work will be cited in the text by book, chapter, and paragraph. Quotations are taken from Volume 11 of *A Select Library of the Nicene and Post-Nicene Fathers of the Christian Church,* ed. Philip Schaff.

exempt the Christian faith from the laws of learning. *Second,* it is self-refuting, for if men were taught directly by God without the need of helps, aids, books or lectures, then those who held this doctrine would not have to teach it. All Christian men would know it. It does not make logical sense to use ordinary methods of teaching to demonstrate that ordinary methods of teaching are inadequate. *Third* (here lies the main weight of Augustine's refutation), three things are necessary for the correct interpretation of sacred Scripture: piety, fear, *and* knowledge. Piety and fear represent the psychological or spiritual prerequisites for the understanding of Scripture. But in themselves they are not enough. Knowledge is just as necessary. The reason is that the Scriptures touch upon certain matters which are the concern of secular studies. History is one such example. If the interpreter of Scripture is to understand the historical elements of Scripture he must know something about history. Piety and fear are here no substitute for learning.

Augustine's thesis may be put in this form: *If we are to interpret Scripture properly, we must be educated in those secular sciences which the Scriptures touch upon.*

Whoever lacks such education and tries to do without it will grasp a tuft of wheat here and there, but he cannot get to the real harvest of Scripture. Therefore first in the order of education must be the liberal arts. But what are the liberal arts?

The Roman educational system reached its highest development in the training of the rhetorician. The rhetorician was more than a technician in speech. His vocation demanded that he be a widely educated person. He had to know the poets, the rules of logic, something about law, and of course much about political theory. Hence he had to study a variety of subjects. This variety was eventually codified into the so-called seven basic liberal arts by Martianus Capella in his work *The Marriage of Mercury and Philology* (fifth century, A.D.). The seven basic liberal arts were divided into the Trivium (grammar, logic, rhetoric) and the Quadrivium (arithmetic, music, geometry, astronomy).

When Augustine lists the subjects in which the Christian scholar must be instructed, he virtually reproduces the curriculum of his training in rhetoric, and matches closely the seven basic liberal arts of the Middle Ages. In short, Augustine attempts to reclaim his education in rhetoric for distinctly Christian purposes. The three purposes of rhetoric in the ancient world were treated by Cicero and were codified by Quintillian. They are to instruct, to move, and to entertain. Augustine adds a fourth: to be used for Christian purposes.[12]

Without stretching the point it may be said that Augustine was the first Christian humanist as well as the founder of medieval scholasticism. E. Harris Harbison calls Augustine's work *On Christian Doctrine* "a classic defense of Christian Humanism,"[13] and G. G. Leckie says his systematic and metaphysical reconstruction of rhetoric made him the "true father of the scholastic tradition which reached its maturity in the thirteenth century."[14]

Augustine's principles in *On Christian Doctrine* thus set the pattern for theological education in the Middle Ages.[15] An ancient woodcut gives us the following picture of medieval education. After learning the rudiments of writing and reading, the student enters the building of education. As he learns the various subjects he mounts higher and higher in the building. He goes from the Trivium to the Quadrivium and up to philosophy, physics, and ethics. At the top of the building is theology, towards which the entire educational process moves.[16] This picture represents rather faithfully the basic theory of Augustine.

12. Cf. G. G. Leckie in his translation of *Concerning the Teacher*, p. xiii.
13. *The Christian Scholar in the Age of the Reformation*, p. 15.
14. *Op. cit.*, p. xi.
15. B. Altaner, an outstanding patrologist, wrote: "Here Augustine attempted a synthesis between Christianity and ancient learning and traced a Christian program of culture which profoundly influenced the development of the following centuries." *Patrology*, p. 510. So also Beryl Smalley, *The Study of the Bible in the Middle Ages* (second edition) , p. 26.
16. In E. P. Cubberly, *The History of Education*, p. 154.

This theory was carried out not only in the medieval period, but also in the time of the Reformation. It is still the educational philosophy behind the German, English, and American theological educational systems. The entrance requirement of an arts degree by American seminaries is faithfully Augustinian.

Thus Augustine would put the liberal arts at the very center of the curriculum of Carthage Christian College.[17] He is not, however, above criticism in his theory. There is no question that his attitude towards the liberal arts is too utilitarian. For him liberal arts are valuable only because they help in the interpretation of Scripture. He fails to see what John Henry Newman saw, that education is to educate the person. Nor did he envision the significance of a liberal arts education for the Christian layman.

But if Augustine believed in the importance of the liberal arts on purely utilitarian grounds, he did not give a crass utilitarian justification. One of the fundamental presuppositions of Augustine's thought is that all truth belongs to God. Where truth is, God is. No theologian in the history of Christian thought has held so vigorously to the union of truth and God as Augustine. If pagans possess truth they possess God's truth. The so-called evil in pagan learning is not in the learning but in the evil use of the truth (II, 36, 54). Therefore Christians have a right to the truth even if it is held by pagan hands. Augustine states emphatically, "Let every good and true Christian understand that wherever truth may be found, it belongs to his Master" (II, 18, 29). "If those who are called philosophers, and especially the Platonists, have said aught that is true and in harmony with our faith, we are not only not to shrink from it, but to claim it for our own use from those who have unlawful possession of it" (II, 40, 60). In yet another strongly worded

17. The early Church was not entirely with Augustine on this. For divergent opinion cf. Harbison, *op. cit.*, and the most valuable article in *Encounter*, XXII (Autumn, 1961), 363-419, by Quirinus Breen, professor of medieval and renaissance history at the University of Oregon.

sentence, he says that Christians must take useful institutions of men and *convert* them to Christian use (II, 40, 60).[18]

What, then, might the proposed curriculum for the Carthage Christian College be, in detail? Augustine places a great emphasis on *language* (II, 11, 16). It was the technical problem of exegesis and translation which focused his attention upon languages. The good theologian must know Hebrew, Greek and Latin. But even here Augustine speaks from principle: *If a discipline requires competence in language for its mastery, then the scholar must learn the languages.* Augustine's principle here has been one of the fundamental ground rules of Western scholarship. A historian who does not know his Latin is doomed to mediocrity if he specializes in the medieval period. No philosopher can achieve greatness in ancient philosophy if he has not learned Greek. Though the larger cultural value we see today in learning the language of another people is perhaps not in Augustine's sight, on the level of technical scholarship his point may not be gainsaid.

But we cannot limit our study of languages merely to the languages themselves. Languages are systems of signs or symbols, and therefore we must know something about signs.[19] Today we call this study "semantics," and it is unfortunate that Augustine is not given his due in contemporary studies in semantics.

18. We must not get the impression that Augustine's interests were entirely bookish. In his work *St. Augustine of Hippo,* Hugh Pope has written a beautiful chapter on Augustine and nature. He cites the following from one of the sermons of Augustine: "Some people, in order to discover God, read books. But there is a great book; the very appearance of created things. Look above you! Look below you! Note it, read it. God, whom you want to discover, never wrote that book with ink; instead He set before your eyes the things that He had made. Can you ask for a louder voice than that? Why, heaven and earth shout to you, 'God made me!' " (p. 249).

19. Augustine was not uninformed of the tremendous importance of semantics or a philosophy of language. His attention in his writings, especially in *On Christian Doctrine* and *The Teacher,* upon signs, i.e., semantics, is proof enough. Cf. Gordon Clark, *Thales to Dewey,* pp. 228-230.

When Augustine leaves the topic of languages and lists other important items he reproduces his rhetorician's curriculum. He lists *music* (II,16,26; II,18,28), *literature* (II,18,28), *civics* (11,25,39), *history* (II,28,42; II,28,43), *natural history* (II,29,45); *astronomy* (II,29,46), *logic* (II,31,48), *science of numbers* (II, 31,48), *rhetoric* (IV,1,2; IV,2,3; IV,3,4), *eloquence* (II,36,54); *geography* (II,29,45), *mechanical arts, shorthand, and writing* (II,26,40), and *comparative religions* — judging from the detailed refutation of Roman religion in the opening chapters of *The City of God*. Lastly, there is *philosophy*, which was implicitly in Augustine's system the best of the contributions of the liberal arts to the service of Christian theology (II,40,60; II,40,61).

We certainly have here more than a basic liberal education. Augustine has been too generous with our time. The content of these subjects is not the same today as it was in Augustine's time. And the standard requirement of most of our contemporary colleges of one laboratory science course is not here specified. But we are interested in Augustine's basic principles. When we look over the core-curriculum of our great universities of today there is not much difference between its list of subjects and Augustine's.

At this point we note three important contributions of Augustine to the Christian Church and Christian education: (i) He showed that a liberal arts education is the best possible prerequisite for the proper understanding of the Christian Scriptures. Someone has said that if a man knows only the Scriptures he does not know the Scriptures. That is, an uneducated mind does not have the proper tools to learn the greatness of the Christian revelation. (ii) He defended a Christian humanism and introduced a problem which the Christian Church and Christian schools have struggled with ever since, namely, how to be thoroughly Christian and thoroughly academic *at the same time*.[20] (iii) He grounded a liberal arts education in the Christian faith. He attempted to create a "comprehensive foundation of a new

20. Cf. F. G. Maier, *Augustin und das antike Rom*, pp. 14-15.

Christian culture"[21] by bringing all cultural activity under the truth of the one true God and putting all knowledge in the service of the faith. There can be no "educated demon" in the educational philosophy of Augustine, for nothing may be admitted into his Carthage Christian College which does not seek faith and love.[22]

(2) *The Carthage Christian College must be expert in diagnosing the unchristian elements in pagan learning*

The ideal in education is instruction in pure truth. But this ideal is beyond us. Education is carried on by fallible professors, fallible students, and with fallible books. There is much error in professor, student, and book. To attribute finality to either professor or book is hence very foolish. A good liberal arts education will therefore convey to the student a keen sense of the fallibility of our finest knowledge.

But Augustine knew that education was complicated not merely by man's finitude and his proneness to error. He knew that man was sinful at the root, and he knew this out of his own experience as well as from Sacred Scripture. And this fact deeply affects human learning. The subjects of the liberal arts will suffer not only from man's imperfections (hence they are always liable to correction), but much more from his corrupting depravity. Accordingly, there will be many unchristian elements in these materials. Carthage Christian College must be very shrewd in its understanding of human knowledge and be able to distinguish unchristian elements in even the best products of human scholarship. Not to think this way is to repudiate in principle the Christian doctrine of sin, and to defend a neo-paganism which asserts that the only errors in human knowledge are errors of judgment or errors of fact.

By way of illustration we note that Augustine warns "studious and able young men, who fear God and are seeking for happiness

---

21. *Ibid.,* p. 29.
22. Maier thus comments: "This devaluates all classical culture not only in its object but also in its innermost drive." *Loc. cit.*

of life, not to venture heedlessly upon the pursuit of the branches of learning that are in vogue beyond the pale of the Church of Christ, as if these could secure for them the happiness they seek; but soberly and carefully to discriminate among them" (II,39,58). Some modern educators have taken exception to this advice of Augustine on the grounds that such fears soon involve the heavy hand of church censorship. But this criticism avoids the question of man's depravity; if man is a sinful creature he cannot rush into anything without first reckoning with the possible corruptions of sin within it. In another passage Augustine tells us that the Christian is to test pagan learning with Scripture: if Scripture censures it, he is to censure it; if it is useful, then it is already approved in Scripture (II, 42,63). The point here is that the Christian makes a *critical* use of pagan learning, and he does so from a Christian perspective. The pagan is uncritical of his own learning, at least uncritical of its distortion from his own depravity. The Christian who rejects all pagan learning errs, because he thereby rejects that measure of God's truth found in it; on the other hand, the Christian who uncritically accepts all pagan learning also errs, because he thereby accepts that measure of untruth found in it.

It was not difficult for Augustine to spot the more obvious unchristian elements in pagan culture. He knew that it was riddled through with astrology (II,22,33) and other superstition (II,17,27). He was suspicious of Roman art because it embodied immoral themes and polytheistic motifs (II,25,39). In the first part of *The City of God* he takes full measure of Roman religion, and finds it wanting at a number of points. A thinker imbued with the Christian doctrine of the spirituality, holiness, unity, and triunity of God could not but rebel violently against Roman religion.

Augustine reveals a critical spirit in all of this. Like Paul he holds that everything is to be judged from the knowledge of God revealed in Jesus Christ (II Cor. 10:4-6), and wherever one finds the true, the honorable, the just, the pure, the lovely, the gracious, the excellent, and the worthwhile (Phil. 4:8) he is to think on these things with approval. Augustine believed in astronomy but not in astrology; he accepted the course of nature as ordered of God, yet he would have no commerce with Roman magic; he took the Platonists as the best guides in philosophy but they were no substitutes for the Biblical writers. Augustine refused to be pushed into any corner. He refused to be the Fundamentalist of the early Church by refusing to negate the truth in classical learning, and at the same time he refused to be the Erasmus of the early Church by refusing to value his Latin learning as greater than Christian revelation. Augustine was a consistent Christian humanist whose Christianity was deeper than his humanism.

Augustine saw not only the obvious unchristian elements in the Roman way of life but also the fundamental contradictions in paganism and its learning. Although other Church Fathers had been critics of Roman culture, Augustine was the first to diagnose its weaknesses profoundly, predict its collapse, and announce the impossibility of its regeneration.[23]

To understand this phase of Augustine's thought we must reflect upon two previous statements we have made about Augustine: first, Augustine was thoroughly trained in the educational system of the Latin world. He knew his Cicero, Varro, Sallust, Horace, Ovid, Persius, Terence, Callustus, and Virgil. He taught rhetoric for one year at Tagaste, eight years in Carthage, one year in Rome, and two years in Milan. William Barclay's observation is that Augustine, "apart altogether from his Christianity, was one of the great scholars of his day."[24] Second, he did not repudiate pagan learning but reasoned that just as the Israelites spoiled the Egyptians and took with them Egyptian gold and silver, so Christians should not repudiate secular learning but carry away as much as is consistent with

23. Two works which go into great detail concerning Augustine's masterful criticism of his own Roman culture and learning are: C. N. Cochrane, *Christianity and Classical Culture,* and F. G. Maier, *Augustin und das antike Rom.*
24. *Educational Ideals in the Ancient World,* p. 213.

Christian perspectives. Augustine sought a critical reconciliation of classical learning with Christianity. Of course, at the point of life-perspective, or basic presuppositions, there was no common ground. The Roman way of life was destined to death and Augustine could not identify himself with it. He was incensed with the immorality of its literature, its excitation of the sensual, and its portrayal of the gods, especially in its mythology. Therefore he advocated a reconciliation made on the basis of the Christian faith, not an amalgamation, syncretism, or uncritical assimilation made on some third and neutral basis. He aimed at a new culture, a Christian culture, which would be formed by the Christian life-impulse but which could critically salvage all the worthwhile elements in the ancient learning. Only a life-view built upon Christian revelation could avoid the vanity and superficiality which plague all purely human systems.

Christian colleges today are called to the same role. We, too, must be critics of our own culture and our own educational world. We would be very naive and very unfaithful to our Christian faith if we were to believe that in the twentieth century no marks of human depravity could be found in our culture or in our education. We, too, are called upon to engage in the kind of profound cultural and educational criticism exhibited by Augustine. We, too, must show that our Christianity is deeper than our humanism — even more pointedly, deeper than the speciality in which we have earned our advanced degrees.

Like Augustine's, this criticism must be profound, not simpleminded. A devil's mask often conceals truth. For example, an outright attack on Freud in the name of Christian morality might miss the insight Freud can give us into the comprehensive nature of our sexuality. In our attempt readily to rid ourselves of Hume, Nietzsche or Voltaire, we may overlook the terrible call to honesty in Christian theology which comes from such men. God does not always whip us with a branch from the tree in the church yard. We must not prejudge God's correctives as Israel did, much to her dismay. Our criticism of our culture, therefore, must never be cheap, never artificial, never naive.

But we must be critical. If we are not critical we remain pagan in our mentality, even though we may teach in a Christian school and affiliate with a Christian church.[25] We cannot overlook the possible manifestations of man's wickedness in every subject of the arts and the sciences. If professors in Christian colleges are to be true to its charter they must engage in such competent cultured criticism. Revelation is given not only to shed light upon the way but to give us perspectives from which we can interpret and criticize. Romans 1:16ff. is an apostolic example of cultural criticism from a Christian perspective.

(3) *The Carthage Christian College must magnify the greatness of the Christian revelation.*

It is difficult to keep great minds interested in small problems. If small men interpret the Christian faith in a small way, then great men will lose interest in it. In no place is it more important to maintain a great interpretation of the Christian faith than in a Christian college. If a faculty member thinks that the Christian revelation is not really commensurate with the greatness of God, then he will lose interest in Christianity and give it only nominal assent to keep the academic peace. And if the student is given a small interpretation of the Christian faith, he will lose interest in Christianity and consider it irrelevant to much of life. Of all the Christian scholars who have ever lived, none have excelled Augustine in seeing the greatness and the majesty of the Christian revelation. What Augustine said of the oracles of God he could have said of all the great truths of the Christian revelation: "Wonderful is the depth of Thy oracles, whose surface is before us, inviting the little ones; and yet wonderful is the depth, O my God, wonderful is

---

25. Gordon Clark's *A Christian View of Men and Things* is a valuable contemporary example of the Christian as cultural critic from the perspective of Christian revelation. H. Butterfield's *Christianity and History* is a good example of the kind of work a historian can do in the Christian interaction with historical science.

the depth. It is awe to look into it; an awe of honour, and a tremble of love."[26]

The greatness of Augustine as a Christian theologian is precisely that he saw the greatness of the Christian revelation. The result is that he gave it such a great interpretation that he has attracted great men of Western culture for nearly sixteen centuries. And Augustinian scholarship continues today with unabated force. Certainly if Augustine were to direct a Christian college he would tolerate nothing cheap or trivial in the Christian understanding of things; he would call student body and faculty to see the Christian revelation in all its greatness and majesty. Let us spell this out in some detail:

(i) *Augustine saw the greatness of the Christian revelation in personal experience.* His *Confessions* is the story of his life. It has been said that no Greek or Roman could have written an autobiography like this; Cochrane says that Augustine set "a wholly new standard in autobiography."[27]

At this point Socrates and Augustine may be compared. Both men were consumed with a passion for the quest for truth. With Socrates it was the relentless chase of a shrewd intellect that subjected every claim to truth to a powerful dialectical scrutiny. With Augustine it was a terrible thirst of a soul racked in torment until it found the truth. Each man found a radically different resolution in his quest for truth. Socrates found it in a consistent system of logical assertions, or a consistent system of ethical principles; Augustine found it in Jesus Christ and Christian revelation. In Jesus Christ, Augustine found both the divine Logos adumbrated in philosophy, and the divine Saviour adumbrated in the Old Testament Scriptures. And Augustine differs from Socrates in the degree of his thirst, in the religious intensity of his search, and in the fulfillment of his search. Accordingly, as charming as the *Phaedo* and the *Apology* of Socrates are, they cannot compare with Augustine's *Confessions*.

26. *Confessions,* XII, 14, 17.
27. *Op. cit.,* p. 386.

There is another facet to Augustine's quest for truth.[28] Augustine maintained that faith is the beginning of understanding, and that a person cannot truly know something until he has first loved it. Greek rationalism reversed the order: it believed that first we know, then we understand, and then we love. Augustine further maintained that if we are to know anything aright, we must first love God, for love of God is the precondition of knowledge of God, and knowledge of God is the precondition of true knowledge of ourselves and all things. Here is the greatest challenge to the entire Greek and Roman way of life, and here, too, the greatest challenge to the theories of knowledge manifested in contemporary arts and sciences. The Augustinian principle is that our knowledge of God determines the setting of all other knowledge. Therefore our relationship with God is the most fundamental relationship. And therefore *faith* which relates us to God is the precondition of adequate knowledge.[29]

If this be the case, two things immediately follow. *First,* the call to faith is also the call to the fullest possible understanding of God's revelation. Augustine is not calling a moratorium on thought. Quite to the contrary, he is setting forth the conditions in which the mind may truly be itself and view the whole of reality. *Second,* if we do not love God we shall forever be at the edge of truth. We may amass ten thousand pages of accurate technical data in experimental psychology but never come to know the true man made in the image of God. We may completely unravel the mystery of the atom but never know its great Creator. We may become experts in philosophy and know all the technicalities of knowledge but never know the supreme Subject of knowledge, the triune God. And to crown our stupidity we shall view the edge of truth as the center!

Christian experience, to Augustine, is an experience of re-

---

28. For the argument in detail cf. Cochrane, *op. cit.,* pp. 400ff.

29. Cf. "His importance for our purpose is this: in his life and writings he dramatized for future generations of Christian scholars the truth that in all important areas of knowledge a man cannot know unless he believes." Harbison, *op. cit.,* p. 14.

demption. But it is also that fundamental experience which sets us right to know God and all His truth. It is not only profound religious experience but it is profoundly theological and in the right sense philosophical or, better, epistemological. In this Augustine caught the greatness in Christian experience.

(ii) *Augustine saw the greatness of the Christian revelation in its historical dimensions.* It is generally recognized that Augustine created introspective religious literature with his *Confessions* and the Christian philosophy of history with his work *The City of God*.[30] Thus the *Confessions* and *The City of God* complement each other in a remarkable manner. The *Confessions* show the personal intention of the Scriptural history traced out in *The City of God*; whereas *The City of God* shows the objective reference of the great Christian experience of grace traced out in the *Confessions*. Christian theology must be equally interested in sacred history and justification by faith.

One of the probable difficulties in the inner life of a Christian college is that some professors may have a large view of their specialty and a small view of the Christian faith. Consequently their attitude towards Christian revelation is one of condescension: it is a distinct favor to Christianity that they give it some credence. Augustine would not tolerate this for a moment. He would demand that every professor study his Christianity with some of the same scholarly thoroughness he employed in learning his specialty. Only as one learns Christian revelation in some depth can he properly correlate his own specialty with the perspectives of the Christian revelation.

Augustine set the pattern for us with regard to history. He reflected deeply upon Biblical history and Roman history. Augustine may not qualify as a technical historian, but he did find the life-beat of Biblical history and pagan history, and spelled them out with such greatness of understanding that it is impossible even now for a Christian scholar to improve fundamentally upon the basic theses of *The City of God* in regard to a

30. For a comparison of Augustine with the Greek historians Thucydides and Herodotus see Cochrane, *op. cit.,* Chapter XII.

philosophy of history. Because Augustine saw the greatness of the Christian revelation in its historical elements he was able to create *The City of God* with its great interpretation of human history.[31]

(iii) *Augustine saw the greatness of the Christian revelation in its concern for truth.* Augustine's entire life was one passionate quest for truth. Prior to his conversion to Christianity he had sampled some of the leading philosophical options of his times. When these failed, he finally found rest in Christian faith and penned his famous opening lines of the *Confessions*: "Thou movest us to delight in praising Thee; for Thou hast formed us for Thyself, and our hearts are restless till they find rest in Thee" (I,1,1). Having found rest in Christian faith, he did not keep "resting," but probed into the truth of the Christian faith with all the power of his massive intellect. It was out of this restlessness within his Christian rest that he wrote such a monumental theological library. In the *Confessions* he is the master psychologist of religion; in *The City of God* he is the great pioneer in the philosophy of history; in *The Trinity* he is the systematic theologian; in *The Teacher* he is the educational psychologist; in *The True Religion* he is the apologist, and in his anti-Pelagian writings he is the expert controversialist.

Augustine grasped the polychromatic character of the Christian revelation. He saw the fountain of truth in the Christian doctrine of the Trinity; he saw the sum of divine wisdom for human life in the Christian Scriptures; he saw the reality of divine redemption in the incarnation of God in Christ; he saw the participation of man in truth and redemption by the direct illumination of the soul by God; he saw the comprehensive scope of the divine action in his philosophy of history; he saw the depths of human sin in the light of Scripture, using as a foil his own personal experiences and his knowledge of the Roman way of life.

---

31. Cf. Edward R. Hardy, "The City of God," *A Companion to the Study of St. Augustine,* ed. R. Battenhouse, pp. 257-283.

Such a powerful quest for truth and grasp of it is fundamental to Christian higher education. It will be difficult to maintain the Christian faith in its integrity in a proposed Christian college unless, with Augustine, we see the Christian faith in all its greatness, in all its polychromatic truthfulness. If the truth of the liberal arts looks big and the truth of the Christian revelation looks small, it will not be long before the Christian revelation loses its hold on faculty and student body.

Certainly the way is not easy. It demands ability and commitment in administration and faculty. But we do have Augustine before us as an example. Because he saw the Christian faith in its greatness, he became the master of the Middle Ages, the greatest human authority to medieval Christendom. And whenever men wish to study the few great geniuses the human race has produced, they will study Augustine. Let us then attempt to emulate the virtues of this man in our present efforts in Christian higher education.

Lecture II

PHILIP MELANCHTHON (1497-1560):
CHRISTIAN HUMANISM

I. Praeceptor Germaniae

The man who shaped university education in Germany was Luther's friend, fellow professor at Wittenberg, and fellow Reformer — Philip Melanchthon. Because his influence upon German higher education has been so monumental, he has been called the Teacher of Germany (*Praeceptor Germaniae*).

Eleven centuries separate Augustine and Melanchthon. Augustine died in A.D. 430 and Melanchthon in A.D. 1560. We cannot properly assess Melanchthon's educational theories unless we understand certain important matters which developed in those eleven centuries.

(1) *The Roman Catholic Church.*

During these centuries the Roman Catholic Church took its enduring shape. By the time Melanchthon was born it had developed its sacramental system, its body of theology, and its elaborate internal organization. Furthermore, it had created a Catholic way of life — a Catholic value system, a Catholic structured church life, and a Catholic form of piety.

(2) *The University.*

During this period the university came into existence.[1] By

---

1. Cf. C. H. Haskins, *The Rise of the Universities.* The classic is Hasting Rashdall's *Universities of Europe in the Middle Ages* (3 vols.). Cf. also Abraham Flexner, *Universities, American, German, English* and F. Paulsen, *The German Universities.*

Melanchthon's time there was a university tradition of three hundred years' standing. The university was developed from two centers — Bologna in Italy and Paris in northern Europe. The University of Paris was the model for all the German universities. Melanchthon was educated in two such schools, Heidelberg and Tübingen.

(3) Scholasticism.

Scholasticism represents the kind of scholarship produced by the medieval schoolmen (from *scholasticus,* a lecturer). It is a mixture of theology, Latin and Greek classics, philosophy, patristics, and the Latin Vulgate Bible. It had its period of glory, suggested by such names as Anselm and Thomas, but at the time of the Reformation it had greatly degenerated. Part of Melanchthon's problem with Roman Catholicism was the wretched scholarship of the contemporary scholastic tradition.

(4) *The Renaissance.*

In the fourteenth century the Renaissance began in Italy. There were deep cultural, political, and economic forces which caused the Renaissance; by the time of Petrarch (1304-74) it was already gathering momentum. One of the enduring products of the Renaissance was humanism. Humanism stood for two things in particular. (i) It stood for a new set of value judgments. It repudiated the world-denying, self-humiliation, and self-denial representative of medieval Roman Catholic piety. It no longer subscribed to the *via crucis* (the way of the cross), or to the *via dolorosa* (the way of suffering), or to the pietà (the beholding of the crucified Christ). It appreciated a whole realm of values outside the Church, outside the clerical, and outside the religious. (ii) It stood for a new kind of scholarship. The scholastics had known much of the classical literature but the humanists engaged in a radical restudy of the classics, creating the critical means to do this — grammars, lexicons, and critical texts. In the classics they found a source of new values and new moral and spiritual vigor. They experienced a home-sickness (*Heimweh*) for the classical period.[2]

(5) *The Reformation.*

At the beginning of Melanchthon's career as a professor, the Reformation began. Luther produced his famous theses in 1517 and Melanchthon arrived in Wittenberg in 1518. When Luther broke officially with the Roman Catholic Church (December 10, 1520) by burning the papal bull in the presence of faculty and student body, Melanchthon was there. Melanchthon remained true to the cause of the Reformation even though considerable pressure at times was directed towards him to bring him back to the Roman Catholic Church.

Melanchthon was the scholar of the University of Wittenberg and in virtue of this became the educator of the Reformation. Each of the five developments mentioned above contributed to Melanchthon's theory of Christian higher education, which he reconstructed in Germany in harmony with the principles of the Reformation.

II. THE ACADEMIC GREATNESS OF MELANCHTHON

In order to appreciate the educational philosophy of Melanchthon we must first investigate the academic stature of this man.

(1) *His education.*

Melanchthon was a child prodigy. His unusual language gifts were recognized very early in his life. Fortunately, his uncle was John Reuchlin, who was one of the great humanists and Hebrew scholars of the period. Reuchlin guided Melanchthon through his early education, and eventually was the one who recommended Melanchthon to the faculty of Wittenberg.

Melanchthon's first tutor was a thorough Latin grammarian

---

2. Cf. E. G. Schwiebert, *Luther and His Times,* p. 272. Melanchthon's humanism was not the older humanism but the humanism of Erasmus, who profoundly influenced him. Cf. Robert Stupperich, *Der unbekannte Melanchthon,* p. 13.

named Unger who aroused in him a love of Latin. Eventually Melanchthon became the second greatest Latinist of the times, next only to Erasmus. In his later years Melanchthon paid a wonderful tribute to Unger, and said that he was not only a teacher but an academic father, and that it was Unger who made him an expert grammarian.

At the age of thirteen, Melanchthon enrolled at the University of Heidelberg. He studied in lecture and in private reading such subjects as philosophy, rhetoric, astronomy, grammar, dialectics, and under the humanistic influence of the times he read the ancient poets and historians. On June 11, 1511, he received his bachelor's degree. He studied two more years, looking forward to the master's degree which would give him the right to teach, but the Heidelberg faculty considered him too young for the degree. At Reuchlin's advice Melanchthon went to Tübingen, where on January 25, 1514, he received his master's degree. Again he read widely in Greek and Latin literature, philosophy, history, logic, mathematics, and theology. He knew Galen almost by heart.

One very important fact in the development of Melanchthon was that during this period he was influenced by the leading humanists of the times — Erasmus, Reuchlin, Wimpheling, and Agricola. It was this influence which made Melanchthon a Christian humanist. Considering the three factors together (formal education, his private reading, the influence of the humanists), we may draw the conclusion that Melanchthon received the finest education possible in Germany in his times.

(2) *His teaching career.*

Melanchthon's teaching career began as a private lecturer in Tübingen. But the faculty there, firmly settled in a traditionalism and scholasticism, did not find Melanchthon's humanistic philosophy of education suitable, and so, when the opportunity came, Reuchlin recommended him to Wittenberg. When Wittenberg invited Melanchthon to join its faculty, he immediately accepted. The Tübingen faculty did nothing to retain Melanchthon, and so forfeited its chance for academic greatness in that century.

On August 29, 1518, Melanchthon delivered his inaugural address (*Antrittsvorlesung*) before the Wittenberg faculty as the new professor of classics. In it he sketched out his philosophy of higher education, which was in essence the new humanism He knew that the universities were the fountainheads of learning[3] and that whoever won the universities won the battle. From then until his death, Melanchthon was in the thick of university education and the formulation of a philosophy of university education.

His stature as a philosopher of university education may be seen in three aspects.

(i) *He was a lecturer of ability.* The students jammed his lecture hall. One series drew close to two thousand students. And these students came from all the countries of Europe. It is reported that at one time eleven languages could be heard around his supper table.[4] He was also pastor to his students and was always available to them — to discuss the lectures and to hear a recital of their personal problems. He lectured in both the faculties of classics and theology. Consequently he taught a variety of subjects, such as Old Testament, New Testament, theology, Latin and Greek literature, ethics, logic, physics, and metaphysics.

(ii) *He was an author of university texts.* The texts Melanchthon wrote educated German university students for a hundred years.[5] At the age of twenty-one he published a Latin grammar which went through fifty editions and was used by Roman Catholics and Protestants. His work on Terence went into seventy-

---

3. Cf. Clyde Manschreck, *Melanchthon, the Quiet Reformer*, p. 111.
4. Charles Beard, *The Reformation in the Sixteenth Century*, p. 93fn.
5. In his first year at Wittenberg he taught Hebrew and Greek, translated one of Lucian's works, published his work on Titus with a lexicon, completed two works on Plutarch, wrote a dictionary, a Greek hymn, completed a treatise on Athenagoras, one on Plato's *Symposium,* and wrote three volumes on rhetoric! Cf. Manschreck, *op. cit.,* p. 44.

three editions. He also published extensive texts of the Greek and Latin authors — a mere listing of them reads like a *Who's Who* of the classical world — and texts in Greek grammar, physics, and rhetoric.[6]

(iii) *He was an important university administrator.* Melanchthon completely reconstructed the University of Wittenberg in the reorganization of the faculty and the curriculum. Because he had a hand, directly or indirectly, in every university in Germany, he has been called the founder of general learning in Europe.[7] This fact is underscored by one writer who said that "it is not too much to say that the university in all its departments, throughout Protestant Germany, is [Melanchthon's] creation."[8] More than fifty-six cities consulted Melanchthon in the reorganization of their school systems.

Such academic leadership drew the following tribute from Paulsen, the author of a famous work on German university education:

> When Melanchthon died there was probably not a city in Protestant Germany in which some grateful student did not mourn the loss of the *Praeceptor Germaniae.* And long after his death he controlled, through his method and textbooks, the instruction in the Protestant schools and universities. It was primarily due to him that the Protestant half of Germany won ascendancy over Catholicism in the realm of education and culture. There can be no doubt whatever about the final outcome; German philosophy and science, German literature and culture, grew up in the soil of Protestantism.[9]

We cannot but concur in the judgment that "we have to do, then, with no ordinary man in Philip Melanchthon . . . he

6. The enormous number of classical works which Melanchthon eventually edited or translated or commented upon are listed in M'Clintock and Strong, *Cyclopedia of Biblical, Theological, and Ecclesiastical Literature,* VI, 54. Cf. also Paulsen's remark: "For forty-two years (1518-1560) he lectured at Wittenberg on nearly every philosophical, philological and historical subject . . . in his own person representing almost an entire philosophical faculty." *Op. cit.,* p. 43.

7. In Hallam, *History of Literature,* I, 145.

8. Rothe, cited in Manschreck, *op. cit.,* p. 144.

9. F. Paulsen, *op. cit.,* p. 33.

ought to be honored as one of the greatest religious geniuses in the history of the Christian Church since the days of Augustine."[10] If it was Luther who won the masses to the theology of the Reformation, it was Melanchthon who won the educated, cultured, and scholarly people.[11] Certainly the total impact of the Reformation would have been must less without this caliber of convert.

III. MELANCHTHON'S IDEALS FOR A CHRISTIAN UNIVERISTY[12]

We have already noticed that Melanchthon is separated from Augustine by eleven centuries, and that therefore he faced an entirely different cultural situation. But there is yet another marked difference. Augustine could do little to institutionalize his theories of education, though he did work with understudies in his bishopric. Melanchthon, however, had the opportunity to implement his theories first in Wittenberg and then in virtually all of Germany. We have to imagine what Augustine might have said if he had had the opportunity to begin a university, but we may not only read what Melanchthon wrote on education, but because he was administratively in the center of university life we may deduce his ideals from his actual practice. A summary of his ideals for a Christian university follows.

(1) *A Christian university must join in the transmission of culture.*

It was the presupposition of the training of the ancient rhe-

---

10. Dean Flack in the Hill translation of *The Loci of Philip Melanchthon*, p. 32. It should also be mentioned that the famous German gymnasium, the West Point of continental education (when at its best), derived its basic impulse from Melanchthon. Cf. E. C. Helmreich, *Religious Education in German Schools*, p. 20.

11. Cf. "Melanchthon," *Realencyclopedie für protestantische Theologie und Kirche*, 3rd edition, XII, 528.

12. Cf. E. L. Lueker, "Luther and Melanchthon," *Concordia Theological Monthly*, XXI (Aug. 1960), 476-478; R. D. Preus, "Melanchthon the Theologian," *ibid*, 469-475; and C. S. Meyer, "Melanchthon as Educator and Humanist," *ibid.*, (Sept. 1960), 533-540.

torician that he be a widely educated man in order to handle
the variety of situations with which he had to deal. The same
general ideal carried over in the medieval university, for
general knowledge supplied the learning requisite for specialization. The liberal arts training gave the professional man his
necessary cultural background. From this we have the educational truism that the role of a university is to transmit culture.

The Christian Church has had different attitudes towards
culture. The best work that attempts to sketch these different
attitudes is H. Richard Niebuhr's *Christ and Culture*. One of
the recurring attitudes is (in Niebuhr's terms) "Christ against
culture," which we may rephrase into "Christ against liberal
arts education." Put very starkly, the position would amount to
the following: let the state educate its children in liberal arts,
and let the Church educate believers in Biblical and theological
subjects. In the early days of the Bible Institute movement this
attitude was predominant. The only use of liberal arts was
based on very practical considerations. Some English must be
taught and some public speaking and some music, for these
three are very important in the practical communication of the
Christian gospel. But the bulk of the curriculum must be
strictly biblical, theological, and practical.

Melanchthon's total nature would rebel against the notion
that the responsibility of education in liberal arts should be
turned over to pagans. According to Melanchthon the Church
and state face a common set of foes: ignorance, superstition, and
barbarism. The Church had to join in the combat against
these enemies. A Christian institution which does not help
carry its battle against these foes is unworthy of its calling.

Furthermore, the health of the Church is directly related to
the health of the state. No great Christian Church will emerge
from a barbarous, boorish, superstitious culture. Only education drives out barbarism, and if the educational institutions of
the Church do not help in this task, the Church adds to its
own difficulties. It was Melanchthon's strong conviction that

without an educational system a state would lapse into darkness and barbarism.

Furthermore, the health of the state is not dependent solely upon the moral force represented by the Christian ministry. The state needs Christian professional men in all the professions of a culture.[13] These men may have more to do with the health of the state than the ministry itself. The Church, therefore, has no alternative in Christian education but to carry its share in the transmission of culture and in the educating of Christian professional men.

This must be supplemented with one more conviction of Melanchthon. Education was ultimately education only insofar as it was training in ethics. Christian and pagan alike would profit from the ethical instruction inherent in a true liberal arts course. And this common ethical training would reflect itself in a higher ethical standard in the state.[14]

The Christian Church has, then, a real stake in the social order and this stake is protected by an educational system that educates in ethics and helps to transmit the cultural heritage. A Christian university will take upon itself as part of its God-given task the transmission of culture. This emphasis of Melanchthon upon the general salutary effect of education is strongly expressed in his own words as follows:

> Even if we had no souls, and schools and language were not needed for God's sake and the Bible's, there would still be ground enough for establishing the best possible schools both for boys and girls, for the world needs fine and capable men and women to conduct its affairs, that the men may rule land and people wisely and that the women keep house and train their children and servants as they should. Such men are made of boys and such women of girls, and hence it is necessary to educate the boys and girls properly.[15]

It is Melanchthon's insight at this point which is the real refutation of all forms of "Christ against culture." All forms

13. Cf. Manschreck, *op. cit.*, p. 145.
14. Cf. A. Sperl, *Melanchthon zwischen Humanismus und Reformation*, p. 38.
15. Cited by Helmreich, *op. cit.*, p. 14.

of pietism, narrow biblicism, or fanaticism which reject the sharing of culture and its transmission, cripple their own evangelistic efforts. By narrowing their understanding of the Christian faith, they narrow the spread of their evangelistic net, and they restrict the influence of the Christian faith. Christian colleges of the twentieth century had best side with Melanchthon in this issue.

(2) *A Christian university must be a sponsor of the liberal arts as a necessary foundation for competent theological learning.*

Melanchthon's education was a mixture of the later scholasticism and the new humanism. Early in his academic life he became a sharp critic of the later scholasticism and a champion of the new humanism. The old training based on the liberal arts had ceased to be genuine. The method of disputation at the center of later scholasticism did not lead to truth but rather to fruitless contentions and to unhealthy desire for victory in debate. Another serious defect was that its scholarship had little interest in source-criticism. Consequently it could perpetuate error from one century to another. For example, with little concern for reading an authority in his own language, a mistranslation of some important passage might go forever uncorrected. With little concern for getting the best possible manuscripts of a writer, and checking them out by critical and historical investigation, a scholar might never know that a given work was spurious.

The remedy for this academic stagnation was a wholesome embracing of the new humanism.[16] Melanchthon indicated his high esteem for humanism when he wrote that "on earth there is nothing next to the Gospel more glorious than humanistic learning."[17] Although both Luther and Calvin profited

---

16. Cf. Sperl, *op. cit.*, p. 32.
17. Cited by Manschreck, *op. cit.*, p. 145. Stupperich's comment is that Melanchthon saw the union of humanism and the Reformation as something given of God. *Op. cit.*, p. 18.

from humanism, it was Melanchthon who cemented humanism into the structure of the Protestant Reformation.

Eby has sketched out for us the common ground of the Reformers and the humanists: (i) opposition to scholasticism; (ii) emancipation of the individual — the Reformers for religious reasons, the humanists for creative and artistic; (iii) admiration of the Latin and Greek classics, which were considered to be sublime treasures of human knowledge; (iv) return to the original documents — the Reformers to the Hebrew and Greek Testaments, the humanists to the Greek and Latin classics; and (v) production of critical literary tools — lexicons, grammars, and critical editions of ancient texts.[18]

Melanchthon's eyes were opened to the deficiencies of contemporary scholasticism when he saw its scholars working with poor texts, bad translations, and at times spurious documents. There was no self-correcting scholarship in all of this. Therefore the new humanism had to be joined to the new theology if the new theology was to avoid the errors of later scholasticism. This marriage is called by Franz Hildebrandt "the dialectical tension between Wittenberg and Athens."[19]

At this point there is a marked parallel between Augustine and Melanchthon. Augustine was a product of the ancient classical period. He incorporated the ancient liberal arts of the rhetorician into his educational philosophy because the meaning of Sacred Scripture can be gained only against a wide educational background. Melanchthon looks backward eleven centuries and more upon the classical period. He sees it as the golden age of the human spirit. A liberal arts education in the classics has more than a pragmatic value. Augustine lived in the period of the decline and senility of the classical period, hence his attitude is that of pragmatically salvaging what he could from it. To Melanchthon, however, the classical liberal arts

18. F. Eby, *The Development of Modern Education* (second edition), pp. 40-42.

19. *Melanchthon: Alien or Ally?* p. 3. This is a play on Tertullian's famous remark, "What has Jerusalem to do with Athens?"

were the means to the education of the total person. Through the education of the complete person comes the improvement of the cultural and social condition of the state. Accordingly, Melanchthon sees a threefold value in a university education centered in the classics: (i) the high ethical standards of the best of the classics instruct the students in ethical living;[20] (ii) education in the classics produces an ethical and cultured person, and the state is enriched by every person so educated; (iii) education in the classics is the best possible education for the ministry.

Melanchthon is particularly concerned with the education of the Lutheran minister. He was most insistent that this man be educated in the liberal arts and according to the standards of the new humanism. It was axiomatic with Melanchthon that the fate of theology hung upon the fate of the liberal arts.[21] If the liberal arts fell to a low level, then theology would fall to the same low level. Therefore liberal education must be kept at the foundation of theological education *at all costs.*

It was Melanchthon's opinion that theologians without a humanistic education had only one eye. The theologian who did not have the second eye of training in liberal arts would inevitably blunder. For example, without proper training in rhetoric he could not interpret the Scriptures properly, for a knowledge of rhetoric is fundamental to the proper interpretation of Scripture. Lacking in philosophy and logic, the theologian could not put together a decent argument, for only by the study of logic can the theologian or preacher learn the pitfalls of faulty logic. A theological argument constructed by a person not trained in logic would inevitably reflect this lack. This union of humanism and evangelical theology — learned piety — was characteristic of every Protestant university which came

20. In his inaugural lecture (*Antrittsvorlesung*) he said that the goal of education was the knowledge of nature and the ethical-cultural education of the self (*sittliche Persönlichkeitsbildung*). As we shall see later, he is one with Newman at this point.
21. Cf. Sperl, *op. cit.,* p. 29.

directly or indirectly under the influence of Melanchthon.[22]

Melanchthon, however, did not always have his way. Even at Wittenberg, it was a lifelong struggle to maintain intact his formula of learned piety. The intense theological atmosphere of the Reformation kept crowding the liberal arts. But he would not give up his insistence upon their importance. He came to Wittenberg as a professor in the faculty of classics, but found himself drawn also into the faculty of theology. He resolutely refused, however, to give up his chair in classics and devote his energies entirely to theology. He sensed that a relaxing of zeal for learning in classics would shortly involve loss of interest in Hebrew and Greek. If this happened, then the students could make no real progress in theology; their effort would be like trying to fly without feathers. Therefore he found it necessary to oppose Luther. He could not allow theology to swallow up the liberal arts.[23] Consequently he kept up his work in classics by lecturing and by issuing a constant stream of critical editions of ancient texts. His basic philosophy was that man proceeded from knowledge to piety, and that if a man neglected his knowledge he would soon lose his greatness in piety.[24]

To sum up, Melanchthon believed that the new humanism was the means of recovering the genuine value of the historic liberal arts. University education was to be grounded in humanism because it was the best possible foundation for the professional men so necessary for a healthy state, and the proper foundation for theological education. If the liberal arts suffered deterioration, then the individual, the state, and the Church would each suffer.

Turning now from Melanchthon's general theory of the role

---

22. Cf. Manschreck, *op. cit.*, p. 97. There was yet another reason for the minister's education in liberal arts. The Reformation put a premium upon theology and therefore the minister needed the training adequate for this task. The result was that the theological faculty was the most important in the German universities of the sixteenth and seventeenth centuries. Cf. Paulsen, *op. cit.*, p. 51.

23. Cf. Beard, *op. cit.*, p. 90.

24. Cf. Flack, *op. cit.*, pp. 40-41.

of the new humanistic learning, let us examine its specific application, sampling three disciplines in particular:

(i) *Philology*. Melanchthon was certain that the foundation of education must be competence in languages. His conviction stemmed from his concern for good scholarship and for a true knowledge of the Scriptures. A scholar, Melanchthon believed, must know the original language of the materials he works with in order to work competently with them. He saw again and again in the scholarship of his times the evils of inability to work in the original languages of the documents. The only corrective to error was a method of scholarship which was self-correcting. In regard to the Scriptures, Melanchthon's argument was as follows. The doctrine of justification by faith means that every person is justified immediately by God without the sacramentally graced Church or the sacramentally empowered priest. This immediacy of the divine action implies the ability of every man to read for himself the Scriptures, wherein the gospel of the grace of God is documented. But reading the Scriptures presumes a basic education. Therefore, each man, from ploughman to scholar, must have that reading skill necessary for his station in life.[25] Justification by faith means a universal education among the people so that all may read the Christian Scriptures, and it means the scholarly knowledge of Hebrew and Greek by the theologians and ministers.

The Hebrew and Greek Testaments, however, cannot be picked up like the latest newspaper and be immediately read and understood. They are records from ancient cultures with strange histories. Therefore the scholar must know more than Hebrew and Greek grammar. He must know all the sciences necessary for the reconstruction of a culture now deceased. Melanchthon wrote the following on this point: "Without an understanding of language, one cannot read the Old and New Testaments; and to understand language one needs all sorts of related knowledge in history, geography, chronology and other liberal arts."[26] There-

---

25. See Helmreich, *op. cit.*, p. 7, and Manschreck, *op. cit.*, p. 132.
26. Cited by Manschreck, *op. cit.*, p. 146.

fore the University of Wittenberg cannot offer Hebrew and Greek and let it go at that! The entire range of liberal arts must be taught as the necessary background for the proper use of the ancient languages. Therefore the new humanism was the friend of good theology.[27]

Years of training are required to develop the skills necessary for the proper translation of ancient documents. Not only must the cultural period of a given document be mastered, but the details of the grammar of the languages as well. Melanchthon was consequently a stickler for grammar. "Every theologian and faithful interpreter of heavenly doctrine must necessarily be first a grammarian, then a dialectician, and finally a witness."[28] This emphasis upon grammar, however, was not pedantic. Grammar was the instrument whereby the scholar gained the treasures of an ancient document of the classics or the Christian Scriptures.[29]

The practical outcome of all of this is that the classical studies, along with Latin, Greek and Hebrew, must be the heart of the curriculum in a Christian university. Here Melanchthon and Augustine thoroughly concur. Even Martin Luther must be resisted, for he threatened to let theology overpower the classics.[30] The reason why Melanchthon opposed even Luther at this point is explained in his own words:

> The languages are the scabbard in which the Word of God is sheathed. They are the casket in which this jewel is enshrined; the cask in which this wine is kept; the chamber in which this food is stored . . . . If through neglect we lose the languages (which may God forbid), we will not only lose the Gospel, but it will eventually come to pass that we will lose also the ability to speak and write either Latin or German.[31]

27. Cf. Hansjörg, *Melanchthon als Ausleger des Alten Testaments*, p. 44.
28. Cited in "Melanchthon," *The New Schaff-Herzog Encyclopedia of Religious Knowledge*, VII, 283.
29. Cf. Manschreck, *op. cit.*, p. 147.
30. *Ibid.*, p. 146.
31. Cited by Helmreich, *op. cit.*, p. 14.

(ii) *Rhetoric.* It has already been noted that training in rhetoric was the equivalent of a university education in the Roman empire. The gains in rhetoric were carried over into the Middle Ages in the form of the seven liberal arts, and in the study of the great rhetoricians of antiquity (e.g., Aristotle, Demosthenes, Cicero, Quintilian). Melanchthon was immersed in this tradition and wrote his own text on the subject (*Elements of Rhetoric*).

According to Melanchthon, rhetoric is a double help to the theologian. *First,* it sharpens his mind. In rhetoric the student studies a very elaborate set of rules. The sheer exposure to such a set of rules cannot help but sharpen the wits of the theological student. Reading between the lines we infer that one of Melanchthon's fears was that a theologian would disgrace himself in the academic community by his poor logic or badly constructed argument, by not having his wits about him. A stiff training in rhetoric prevents this. *Second,* rhetoric is essential for the understanding of Scripture. The student of rhetoric learns how speeches are composed. The interpretation of much of Scripture is the interpretation of speeches. If the student knows how these are constructed, he is well on his way to knowing how to interpret them. Therefore the preacher expertly trained in rhetoric is already a good interpreter of the Scriptures.[32]

(iii) *Philosophy.* The service of philosophy to theology is similar to that of rhetoric. Philosophy supplies the theologian with the critical apparatus necessary for good theology. To neglect philosophy and logic in the name of piety is not to achieve better piety but, rather, more stupidity.[33] Logic gives the theologian skill in method, order, definition, division, proper connection, and real association. Without these skills, the theologian will mangle the truth. To use Melanchthon's own analogy, such professed avoidance of the wisdom of the

32. Cf. Hansjörg, *op. cit.,* p. 42.
33. Cf. Manshreck, *op. cit.,* p. 96.

world produces men who tear up the truth of God like a puppy tears up rags.

The theologian skilled in philosophy can thereby present his theological arguments in proper form. They will be orderly, logical, and plausible expositions. But there is still another advantage in knowing philosophy. The theologian skilled in logic can spot the sophistry in the argument of his opponent.

Luther and Melanchthon did have some differences of opinion about the role of philosophy. Luther was much angered with philosophy, for he saw the bad use made of Aristotle by the Roman Catholic theologians. For this reason he called Aristotle a damned rascally heathen, and reason the devil's whore.[34] On the contrary, Melanchthon saw that Aristotle could be used by Christians with profit. The fact of the matter was that the theologian who knew his Aristotle would be a better theologian than the one who didn't.

Melanchthon's use of philosophy was a critical one. He did not follow the scholastics who bodily incorporated some philosophy into their theology. He viewed philosophy more as a critical function than as a system-building activity. Flack thus maintains that Melanchthon anticipated the contemporary mood in philosophy which sees philosophy not as system-building but as the criticism of the arts and sciences.[35]

We have now surveyed Melanchthon's thesis that a Christian university should supply the background for theological training.

34. "Whore of the devil," "devil's bride," "the beautiful harlot." Cited and documented in G. Forell, *Faith Active in Love*, pp. 53-54fn. Forell also cites the very complimentary statements Luther made about reason (p. 54). Draper cites Luther on Aristotle (without documentation) as follows: "truly a devil, a horrid calumniator, a wicked sycophant, a prince of darkness, a real Apollyon, a beast, a most horrid impostor on mankind, one in whom there is scarcely any philosophy, a public and professed liar, a goat, a complete epicure, this twice exorable Aristotle." *History of the Conflict between Religion and Science*, p. 215. In *An Open Letter to the Christian Nobility* Luther had called Aristotle a "damned conceited rascally heathen." *Works of Martin Luther*, II, 146.
35. Flack, *op. cit.*, p. 42. Whether Melanchthon admitted too much of Aristotle back into theology after Luther had evicted him is yet another problem.

This is in harmony with Augustine's theses and in harmony with the better educational philosophy of the Middle Ages. It has had a sustained verification in the history of theological education since the Reformation. Attempts to educate for the Christian ministry while bypassing the liberal arts result in self-defeat. Such an education cannot produce a great expositor of Scripture. It cannot produce the learned theologian. It cannot produce the minister who can minister to every stratum of society. It would be safe to say as a general observation that the properly educated minister of the gospel of Christ can minister to the rich and the poor, to the noble and to the humble, to the cultured and to the ignorant. But in most cases the poorly trained man can minister only to the poor, ignorant, and uncultured. A theological education which short-cuts the liberal arts ends up in short-cutting the effectiveness of the ministry, short-cutting the effectiveness of the Christian Church, short-cutting the evangelistic and missionary work of the Church, and short-cutting the serious and wonderful labor of the theological disciplines.[36]

(3) *A Christian university courageously bears its witness in the academic community.*

Melanchthon's formula was learned piety. Learning must lead to piety. Piety without learning snuffs out the candle of truth, and learning without piety is but educated paganism. Quintilian, the great systematizer of Roman rhetoric, had insisted that the good orator must be a good man:

> The perfect orator must be a man of integrity, the good man . . . and we therefore not only require of him a consummate talent for speaking, but all the virtuous endowments of the mind . . . not only that the orator ought to be a good man; but that he cannot be an orator unless such.[37]

36. Melanchthon said it in these words: "My whole purpose in life has always been twofold: to stimulate others to cultivate *bonae literae* and to bring the study of *bonae literae* into harmony with theology." Meyer, *op. cit.*, p. 536.

37. Cited by R. R. Rusk, *The Doctrines of the Great Educators*, p. 39.

Melanchthon fully accepted this ancient ideal and carried it over into his philosophy of university education. To it, he added his own Christian belief. Learned piety meant the study of ancient classics and Christian theology. University education rooted itself in the classics, but crowned itself in Christian faith. Melanchthon consequently defended a Christian humanism.[38] His humanism was never for its own sake, but for the gospel's sake. This union of humanism and evangelical faith still characterizes education in the German, Swiss, and Scandinavian universities, despite departures from the theology of the Reformers.

Melanchthon was formally the first theologian of the Reformation. Luther was the passionate prophet, although his scholarly abilities must not be minimized; his Bible translation, his Reformation tracts, and his commentaries establish his ability as a scholar. But it was Melanchthon who became the theologian and then the educator. His *Loci Communes* and the *Augsburg Confession* were of incalculable influence in the course of the Reformation. Melanchthon as humanist, professor, educator did not fail to register his Christian convictions.

This did not come easy for Melanchthon. Manschreck calls him the "quiet Reformer." By disposition Melanchthon was the scholar and not the crusader. His nature was mild and conciliatory. He had little zest for religious controversy. Left to his natural inclinations he would have followed the life of the specialist in classics. But Melanchthon was a man of faith, and when the situation called for it he stood for the faith at the severe cost of his internal disposition.

The greatness of Melanchthon at this point can be measured by the behavior of Erasmus and Reuchlin. Both were humanists; both were experts in their speciality, Erasmus in Greek and Reuchlin in Hebrew. They were called the eyes of Germany. But they were humanists first and Christians second. This can be seen in Erasmus, whose *Praise of Folly* shows that he knew the corruption of the times. Yet to him the dogmatic was secondary in religion and he perferred Roman Catholic dogma to Protestant dogma. Consequently, both men avoided all ecclesiastical conflict by remaining nominal members of the Roman Catholic Church. This meant that Melanchthon was faced with a painful decision. He had to part company with Erasmus, and — even more painful — he had to part company with Reuchlin. Reuchlin was his academic father. He had taught Melanchthon Hebrew; he had supervised his education; he had obtained his post at Wittenberg. If Melanchthon sided with Luther it would cost him Reuchlin. Nevertheless, when confronted with the decision of siding with the truth of the Lutheran Reformation or siding with his beloved uncle, Melanchthon stood with Luther and the purification of the Christian faith. And so he wrote to Reuchlin: "Many things call me to you — the desire to be near you, love of home, the prospect of association with many learned men, a wonderful library to use, and my health . . . . [But] I ask not to live happily but righteously and Christlike."[39]

Reuchlin had intended that his library go to Melanchthon, but in bitterness over Melanchthon's siding with Luther he willed his library to the monks of Pforzheim. Furthermore, he requested Melanchthon that he not write to him for fear that he be taken as a heretic. Manschreck is right when he says that "nothing could more forcefully have indicated the commitment of Melanchthon to the evangelical reform movement, nor demonstrated so effectively that humanism was not his final standard."[40]

To understand better the situation in which Melanchthon found himself and made his decision, we must look back to Luther and the University of Wittenberg. When Luther came to Wittenberg, he found a faculty entrenched in the stagnant

---

39. Cited by Manschreck, *op. cit.,* p. 53.
40. *Loc. cit.* Luther and Erasmus had a strong theological falling out over the freedom of the will. Melanchthon wrote kindly and affectionately to Erasmus but stayed with Luther.

scholasticism of the period. Markedly influenced by the new humanism, Luther effected a complete reversal of the educational philosophy of the school. By 1518 the entire faculty espoused the new Biblical humanism of Luther.[41]

When Melanchthon came to Wittenberg he, too, was a disciple of the new humanism. Under the influence of Luther, he also became a disciple of the new *Biblical* humanism. Luther gained much for himself and for his movement from the great learning of Melanchthon, and Melanchthon gained the newfound faith of the Reformation from Luther. And so was formed their friendship, one of the most remarkable in the history of the Reformation. On one occasion Luther said: "I would sooner die than be separated from this man,"[42] and in a famous passage he describes the difference between himself and Melanchthon:

> I am rough, boisterous, stormy, and altogether warlike. I am born to fight against innumerable monsters and devils. I must remove stumps and stones, cut away thistles, and thorns, and clear the wild forests; but Master Philip comes along softly and gently sowing and watering with joy, according to gifts which God has abundantly bestowed upon him.[43]

Every scholar is called to the same decision as Melanchthon. Melanchthon was Christian first, humanist second. He saw that the issue of the Gospel was greater than any particular issue in scholarship, and he had the moral courage to stand for Jesus Christ. He is thus an example for scholars today in Christian colleges. Let them be Christian first and scholars second. Otherwise they declare that in principle the Christian faith is trivial.

---

41. E. G. Schweibert, *op. cit.*, p. 293 ("Luther Wins the Wittenberg Faculty").
42. *Realencyclopädie*, XII, 528.
43. Cited by Manschreck, *op. cit.*, p. 54. It is said that Luther prevented Melanchthon from becoming a second Erasmus. From time to time Melanchthon was put under great pressure by the Catholics to entice him back. But he stood true to Luther and loyal to the theology of the Lutheran Reformation.

Lecture III

JOHN HENRY NEWMAN (1801-1890):
A CATHOLIC OXFORD

I. THE MAN

John Henry Newman was one of the finest products of nineteenth-century England. No matter which way we turn in the cultural history of England, we run into this man. Most selections of English literature include something from his autobiography, *Apologia pro vita sua*. A survey of British philosophy of the nineteenth century must reckon with the theory of knowledge contained in his *The Grammar of Assent*. No serious student of theology can conscientiously bypass his *Essay on the Development of Christian Doctrine*. And certainly one of the few great works of all centuries on the character of university education is his work *The Idea of a University*.

Newman was also deeply involved in the ecclesiastical history of the century. He was one of the leaders of the Oxford Movement, or Tractarian Movement, which attempted a renewal of the Church of England. His conversion to the Roman Catholic Church was certainly the most crucial in the religious history of the period. Finally, Newman's sermons preached in St. Mary's, Oxford, were among the finest of the day and exerted an influence in all of England.

There was something unique about the personal presence of Newman. He was deeply mystical in nature, and this was communicated by his very presence in any room or gathering. He carried this same mystical aura into the pulpit, and it added immensely to the power of his masterful English style. The reader catches something of this mystical quality even in the printed page of Newman. His mastery of the English language marks him as one of the great English stylists of his century.

Newman commenced his theological and academic career when he entered Trinity College in Oxford in 1817. He was later elected a fellow of Oriel College, in 1822, which was in itself no small honor. He was called to be principal of Alban Hall in 1825 and in 1828 he became vicar of St. Mary's in Oxford.

Newman was the early leader of the Oxford Movement (so named because it had its origin at Oxford University), also called the Tractarian Movement (because it propounded its theses in a series of tracts). It was a movement which attempted to revitalize the Church of England in its theology, in its appreciation of its historical heritage, and in its spirituality. Newman gave this movement the inspiration of his person and the strength of his pen. As he kept writing, reading, and pondering, however, he came to the conclusion that Anglicanism was inconsistent Roman Catholicism and that to be true to itself it ought to reunite with the Roman Church. This spiritual and intellectual struggle of the Anglican versus the Roman Catholic in Newman came to an end on October 9, 1845. On this rainy, wintry evening, Newman found his way to a Roman Catholic institution in Oxford, fell exhausted on his face before Father Dominic, and asked for admission into the Roman Catholic Church. The drama is recited by Newman in his famous autobiography, *Apologia pro vita sua*, which ranks close to Augustine's *Confessions* in the literature of religious autobiography.

II. The Educator

Newman's entire life was one of academics and scholarship. In his *Journals* he wrote that "from first to last, education, in the large sense, has been my line,"[1] and in commencing his famous lectures on the idea of a university he confessed that

1. Cited by F. De Hovre, *Catholicism in Education.* Four chapters are devoted to Newman's educational theories.

he had "lived the greater part of [his] life in a place which has all that time been occupied in a series of controversies among its inmates and with strangers, and of measures, experimental or definitive, bearing upon [liberal arts education]."[2]

In particular his was an Oxford education. We have already mentioned his education at Oxford, his honors at Oxford, and his vicarage in a church in Oxford. Although he lived away from Oxford after his conversion to the Roman Catholic Church, he never got Oxford out of his blood. One of the most touching scenes of his life was on the day in 1877 when, seventy-six years old, he was elected an honorary fellow of Trinity College of Oxford.

The historical incident which drew Newman directly into the issues of university education was the desire of the Roman Catholic Church to found a Catholic university in Ireland. The educational situation in Ireland at the time was disadvantageous to the Catholics, and therefore the bishops of the Church thought it necessary to have a Catholic university. Newman was selected to be the rector of this university, and he spent four years in Dublin. Circumstances, however, were against him and the project failed. For one thing, there was too much internal politics in the Roman Catholic hierarchy. But in spite of the university's failure, Newman's lectures were a great success. They form one of the few great contributions to the philosophy of a university education.

It is not our purpose to reproduce the complete educational theory of Newman. Our concern is with his philosophy of a Christian university. As in previous discussions, we shall ask the question: What are Newman's principles for a Christian university?

III. THE COMPONENTS OF A CHRISTIAN UNIVERSITY

After poring over Newman's thoughts, trying to reckon how he would formulate a basic set of rules for a Christian uni-

2. *On the Scope and Nature of University Education,* p. 1 (the heart of the larger work, *The Idea of a University*).

versity adaptable to the American scene, we feel the following to be the cardinal ones:

(1) *A university is Christian if it grants theology full rights in the curriculum and if theology receives full respect in all faculties.*

Newman's education at Oxford occurred when the classical curriculum was still the main staple of one's education. However, a revolution, in the making since Galileo,[3] was approaching. Soon science would no longer be the work of rarely gifted men working in their own laboratories, but would burst unceremoniously, like a long-legged teen-ager, into the quiet halls of the old universities.

This revolution forced itself on the academic community between the time Newman finished his studies at Oxford and the time he was called to commence the university at Dublin. The first symptom was the new scientific and empirical mentality of many philosophers. This new philosophical spirit was rooted in the sciences, and it started to push and crowd the entrenched forms of idealism. Newman was aware of this new mood exemplified by John Stuart Mill and Auguste Comte. The second symptom was more concrete than that of general philosophical outlook. Newman writes: "It is the fashion just now, gentlemen, as you very well know, to erect so-called universities, without making any provision in them at all for theological chairs."[4] But this was not the only severe blow dealt to the traditional notion of a university. Adding insult to injury, the scholars in the other departments of the universities simply ignored theology and carried on their specialized labors as if nothing could be said to them from the science of theology.

The Oxford of Newman's undergraduate days was corroding

3. Cf. Crane Brinton, *The Shaping of the Modern Mind;* J. H. Randall Jr., *The Making of the Modern Mind* (second edition); and E. A. Burtt, *The Metaphysical Foundations of Modern Science.*

4. *On the Scope and Nature of University Education,* p. 9.

before his eyes, for it, too, underwent an educational reform, and a new spirit pervaded the campus — a secular, naturalistic spirit. And a new breed of scholar was walking the time-worn paths — the biologist, the chemist, the geologist.[5]

The critical issue in the revolution of university education was clearly (in Newman's eyes) the status of theology. We can gather the dimensions of this by looking back at the University of Wittenberg. Melanchthon found it a lifelong battle to prevent theology from swallowing up the classics. So intense was the theological atmosphere of the University that at times Melanchthon despaired over the future of classical studies. In Newman's time the situation rapidly reversed itself. It was now theology which must strive with all its might to keep the secular curriculum from crowding it off the campus.

Newman saw the battle and waged war with all the energy of his mind. His strategy, however, was unusual for a theologian. He takes his starting point from the university and not from theology. The purpose of a university, he states, is to teach *universal* knowledge.[6] A university is not a technological institute, nor is it a theological seminary. Institutes and seminaries teach specialized courses and are not therefore universities. But a university by its essence as being a university must teach universal knowledge.

What are we to think of the claim of a university to be a university if it omits one of the major components of universal knowledge? If it does this, it defaults and is not a true university. *If a university omits theology, it has lost its claim to be a university.* Newman's rhetorical question is: "Is it then logically consistent in a seat of learning to call itself a university and to exclude theology from the number of its studies?"[7]

Newman is strongly convinced that theology is a science. He believes that God has so acted in His universe that it is possible

5. Cf. C. H. Harrold, *John Henry Newman,* p. 93.
6. Newman, *op. cit.,* p. xxix.
7. *Ibid.,* p. 10.

for men to have a knowledge of Him. He expresses himself as follows:

> I am not catching at sharp arguments, but laying down grave principles. Religious doctrine is knowledge, in as full a sense as Newton's doctrine is knowledge. University education without theology is simply unphilosophical. Theology has at least as good a right to claim a place there as astronomy.[8]

It was not Newman's intention in his lectures to spell out how we know God. He does not go into any detail concerning the genesis of this knowledge. He presumes it to be there, and if it is there then any university which claims universal knowledge as its province and omits theology has ceased to be truly a university.

A rejoinder might be made that a university has the right to limit its offering and by stipulation it could eliminate theology without doing damage to its character as a university. Newman admits that in some matters we may limit our task through stipulation. But in that a university by its very essence must treat universal knowledge, it cannot stipulate theology out of its curriculum and remain a university.

Another way in which theology may be excluded from the curriculum is to classify religion among the sentiments; if it is merely a sentiment, a subjective choice, an emotional set, then it is not knowledge. Newman lashes out against this thesis of religious liberalism. Newman was a lifelong enemy of such a view, for to him it meant the destruction of Christian dogma and of original Christianity. He counters by saying that the very name of God is itself a theology. One cannot use the name of God *meaningfully* and yet deny that there is such a thing as theology. Deny a knowledge of God, and religion becomes a mere aspect of the universe. To deny a knowledge of God, to classify religion as sentiment, is to make God a constitutional Monarch devoid of all rights and power. Only a fool would make this mistake in religion. But as soon as we

8. *Ibid.*, p. 29.

admit a knowledge of God, then theology cannot be kept out of a university.[9]

If the first evil is the omission of a theological faculty from a new university, the second evil is the attitude of indifference towards theology in the other faculties. Newman paints a compelling picture of the specialist who is so thoroughly dedicated to his task that he cannot take his eyes off his manuscript, or leave his science laboratory to attend chapel.[10] If the theologian seeks conversation with him, he will perhaps feel indignant. "Go away," says the researcher to the theologian. "Pure research is one thing and belief in God is another. We ought not to be foolish and attempt to mix them. I am not a theologian; you are not a scientist. So please do not disturb me, and let us each go our own way."

Newman retranslates this into the following: by this attitude the researcher is affirming that theology is only for those who are interested in the theology; it is not meant for the university classroom; rather, theology is for the parish priest and the catechism class.

In attacking this thesis, Newman's basic argument is that knowledge forms one system. The research professor has not denied that God is, but has relegated the knowledge of God to extra-university functions. But if knowledge forms one system, then no significant section of that system may be excised from the body of knowledge without destroying the unity of knowl-

---

9. The debate yet continues. For a discussion of the issue here raised from the perspective of twentieth-century developments, cf. Helmut Thielicke, *Was ist Wahrheit? Die theologische Fakultät im System der Wissenschaften* (Rede zur Eröffnung der Theologischen Fakultät an der Universität Hamburg, gehalten am 12. November 1954). Thielicke speaks, too, of the complete university (Voll-Universität) but finds this completeness not so much in a full listing of faculties but in an *openness* to all truth, and this includes theological truth. Thielicke, however, is much more sensitive to the special character of theological knowledge and attempts to show that even though theological knowledge is very different from "secular" knowledge, it yet deserves a place in a thoroughly "scientific" institution.

10. *Op. cit.,* pp. 30-31.

edge. Banishing theology from the campus is a mutilation of the unity of truth.

Knowledge has no less an object than the universe and no less a goal than universal knowledge. If the professor admits there is a God, he must admit that God has implicated Himself in the universe; otherwise he does not really believe in God. And if God has implicated Himself in the universe, then universal knowledge must reckon with God in the form of theological science. In short, only as we contemplate God along with our other sciences can we truly contemplate the totality of the universe and become responsible to universal knowledge.

Newman presses hard here against the mentality that wants things both ways. If we assert a belief in God but deny that there is real knowledge of God, our concept of God is meaningless. If we assert that our concept of God is meaningful, then we must affirm the validity of theology. And if we affirm the validity of theology, we must admit it into the curriculum of the university.

To prove his point, Newman gives a long discussion about the psychologist who denies that man has a volitional power. The omission of this one important factor in man destroys the universality of the psychologist's theory. Accordingly, if a man ignores God's action in the universe and attempts to give us a unified interpretation of the universe, this interpretation will be deficient and thereby defective. If we understand what it means to assert the existence of God, we will find it impossible to talk about universal knowledge and ignore the place of theology in this knowledge.

In this connection Newman gives us one of the greatest passages on the being of God in all Christian literature:

> [Theology] teaches of a Being infinite, yet personal; all-blessed, yet ever operative; absolutely separate from the creature, yet in every part of the creation at every moment; above all things, yet under everything. It teaches of a Being who, though the highest, yet in the work of creation, conservation, government, retribution, makes Himself, as it were, the minister and servant of all; who, though inhabiting eternity,

allows Himself to take an interest, and to feel a sympathy, in the matters of space and time. His are all beings visible and invisible, the noblest and the vilest of them. His are the substance, and the operation, and the results of that system of physical nature into which we are born. His, too, are the powers and achievements of the intellectual essences, on which He has bestowed an independent action and the gift of organization. The laws of the universe, the principles of truth, the relation of one thing to another, their qualities and virtues, the order and harmony of the whole, all that exists, is from Him; and, if evil is not from Him, as assuredly it is not, this is because evil has no substance of its own, but is only the defect, excess, perversion, or corruption of that which has. All we see, hear, and touch, the remote sidereal firmament, as well as our own sea and land, and the elements which compose them, and the ordinances they obey are His. The primary atoms of matter, their properties, their mutual action, their disposition and collocation, electricity, magnetism, gravitation, light, and whatever other subtle principles of operations the wit of man is detecting or shall detect, are the work of His hands. From Him has been every movement which has convulsed and refashioned the surface of the earth. The most insignificant or unsightly insect is from Him, and good in its kind; the ever-teeming, inexhaustible swarms of animalculae, the myriads of living motes invisible to the naked eye, the restless ever-spreading vegetation which creeps like a garment over the whole earth, the lofty cedar, the umbrageous banana are His. His are the tribes and families of birds and beasts, their graceful forms, their wild gestures, and their passionate cries.[11]

This is a sample of a description which continues for two more full pages. It shows the profound concept of God which gripped the mind of Newman and explains how strongly he felt against those professors who would banish this God to the local parish catechism class.

And if this is not enough, Newman has yet another arrow in his quiver of arguments against those who would banish theology from the campus. Newman argues that theology is

11. *Ibid.,* pp. 48-49.

not parochial. Theology is not the preoccupation of Protestant or Roman Catholic theologians with a vested interest. On the contrary, theology has been one of the great subjects of human culture. If one reads the ancients — Aristotle, Plato — or if one reads the moderns — Bacon, Locke, Newton, Berkeley, Butler — *he must read theology.* To incorporate theology into the university is not to bring an ecclesiastical subject into the halls of universal learning. Theology has already been there since the days of the Academy and the Lyceum. At fault is not theology but myopic university educators who overlook the great history of theology in the course of higher education, ancient and modern.

Newman now turns in another direction. If God is, and if there is a knowledge of God, then such knowledge cannot "but exert a powerful influence on philosophy, literature, and every intellectual creation or discovery whatever,"[12] and if this is true, theology is a condition of general knowledge, and "to blot it out is nothing short . . . of unravelling the web of university education."[13] Theology bears a relationship to every other science, and therefore when theology is removed from the curriculum the sciences suffer. And they suffer in at least two ways.

If a given science is removed from a university curriculum it does not simply leave a gap; some other science moves into its place.[14] For example, if philosophy were deleted from a university curriculum, the department of psychology would move in and start teaching courses as functional equivalents of the courses in philosophy; or if psychology were pulled out of the catalog, then the philosophy department would move in and start teaching at least the philosophy of learning and philosophical anthropology. Similarly, if theology is dropped out, something functionally takes its place. And that which takes its place

12. *Ibid.,* p. 51.
13. *Ibid.,* p. 54.
14. *Ibid.,* p. 57.

is not only less than theology, but something more than itself. Theology must be kept on the campus so that the various disciplines will maintain their integrity.

Not only must theology occupy its rightful place in the curriculum so that none of the other sciences usurps theology's role and hence loses its own integrity. Theology must be in the university so that the other sciences may benefit from its contributions to the one body of knowledge. Fine arts, painting, sculpturing, architecture, and music need the help of theology, or they become ends in themselves. When painting loses its great religious inspiration, it turns to pagan mythology, and so ministers to our corrupt natures. The composer, unless he is motivated through theology to compose for the glory of God, composes for the glory of himself. Theology has its corrective word for economics. The science of wealth, studied apart from the illumination which theology brings, leads to sin. Unless the economist learns from Scripture the errors into which wealth can lead us, he will not properly interpret the science of wealth. The same is true of medicine. The doctor may inform us that if we wish to preserve our health we must move to the country. This is in the language of ethics a hypothetical imperative. But hypothetical imperatives (if . . . then) are not categorical imperatives. A man may feel called of God to stay in the city and risk his health for the work of the Church. Thus all the advice of doctors must be judged by a man's duty to God. In short, every science needs the insights of theology. If theology is kept off the campus the other sciences will not enjoy these insights. Without these insights, the sciences will stumble into error. Theology alone can maintain the internal integrity of the entire curriculum.

(2) *A university is Christian if and when it produces the Christian gentleman.*

It was the conviction of the great orators of classical antiquity that a proper education made a man a gentleman (Quintilian, Cicero). We have seen that Melanchthon shared this ancient ideal. He saw a moral and ethical power in the study of the ancient classics. This interpretation of the function of education received its finest embodiment in the universities of Oxford and Cambridge. Newman was a product of Oxford and deeply imbibed its ideals. Among the finest definitions of a gentleman that we have are those written by Newman.[15]

The transition in university education in Great Britain was on its way. The liberal arts curriculum was being invaded by the sciences. The atmosphere of culture and classical learning was being replaced by the atmosphere of facts, data, and experimentation. There was also a new goal for education. Education must be *useful*; the university product is no longer the gentleman but the technician.

Here is something that neither Augustine nor Melanchthon faced. Here is a break with a tradition of many centuries. We cannot follow all of Newman's arguments against this new kind of education; rather, we will concentrate on his notion of the gentleman.[16]

Newman stands with Augustine and Melanchthon in considering liberal arts to be the center of university education. The function of this kind of education is to educate the intelligence, to give it powers, graces, attitudes and standards. This educated intelligence Newman calls a philosophical mind. But the creating of the philosophical mind inevitably creates the gentleman. The "liberal knowledge" of the university is identical with the "gentleman's knowledge."[17] In another passage he says that "liberal education makes not the Christian, not the Catholic, but the gentleman."[18]

If utility becomes the end of an education, then education

15. *Ibid.*, pp. 152ff., 181ff.

16. Newman is arguing against the German ideal of a university — the university as center of scientific learning. Newman would relegate scientific research to academies, institutes and private laboratories. He had little idea of the magnitude of the change taking place. Cf. Harrold, *op. cit.*, p. 98.

17. Newman, *op. cit.*, p. 91.

18. *Ibid.*, p. 99.

makes the technician, not the gentleman. If a chemist is thoroughly trained in chemistry but is ignorant of art, philosophy, history, ethics, and literature, then he simply is not educated. Training is not education. There is then no real difference between a baker and a chemist except that the chemist has more skills than the baker. Consider the medical doctor. If the doctor has acquired thousands of facts of anatomy, physiology, pathology and drugs, he cannot be considered educated simply because he has amassed so much data. If the doctor knows nothing of Paul or Plato, Cicero or Shakespeare, then there is no essential difference between the surgeon and the barber except in the technicality of the operation. Education for utility trains technicians, but it does not produce gentlemen. Training and education are different, and unless education produces the philosophical mind, no essential educating has taken place.

Newman does not rule out utility in education. It is a question of what level of utility one is speaking about. Technical training produces an immediate utility, but liberal arts education produces a long-range utility. In that a liberal arts education makes the gentleman, it makes the good citizen, and in making the good citizen, it improves society. *First,* the educated person brings his educated self to any task assigned him and he graces his discharge of that task with the virtues of his education. Other things being equal, the *educated* person will always do a better job than the *trained* person. Therefore the educated person is really more useful than the merely trained person. *Second,* a steady stream of educated gentlemen poured into society exerts a most beneficial influence upon that society. Nothing is truly more useful than this. Concerning this Newman writes:

> But a university training is the great ordinary means to a great but ordinary end; it aims at raising the intellectual tone of society, at cultivating the public mind, at purifying the national taste, at supplying true principles to popular enthusiasm and fixed aims to popular aspirations, at giving enlargement and sobriety to the ideas of the age, at facili-

tating the exercise of political power, and refining the intercourse of private life.[19]

Newman's first nail is now pounded in: the philosophy of utility in education fails because it fails to produce the gentleman and therefore fails in the very substance of education. Now he pounds in the second nail: this gentleman never really comes into his own until he is a Christian gentleman — *a Catholic Christian gentleman.*

Newman has a long section in which he discusses the graces that education bestows upon a man. In some instances an educated person excels even the Christian. Newman is in favor of all the graces education can bestow; but the temptation of the educated gentleman is to turn the graces of his education into his religion. We have already noted that Newman fears that individual disciplines will be developed apart from the insights and correctives of theology. Even so the graces of a liberal arts education can be converted into a religion of culture or a religion of morality and so compete with the truth of God. Bluntly, *education is no substitute for religion,* and however splendid a person a gentleman is, *he is not yet a Christian.* The gentleman becomes a Christian when he is regenerated in "the very depths of the heart."[20] A Christian university cannot have as its goal only the gentleman, but *the Christian gentleman.*[21]

Three observations are in order here about Newman's proposal: (i) Certainly his distinction between training and education is valid. The learning of skills and the amassing of data do not in and of themselves get inside a man and make him different. They do not effect a real alteration in the structure of the man's mentality. They do not put him in touch with the great ideas of the human race as reflected in its literature,

19. *Ibid.,* p. 152. This is one of the finest statements we have on the general cultural ennoblement of university education.
20. *Ibid.,* p. 176.
21. De Plovre (*op. cit.*) devotes an entire chapter to this aspect of Newman's thought (IX). It is a union of the Newman of the Class of 1822 as an Oxford gentleman and the Roman Catholic Newman of 1845.

philosophy, and history.[22]   The technological and utilitarian invasion of our universities has certainly corrupted our notion of what an educated person is.   And the situation is close to incurable when the administrators of a university are themselves products of a university system which has lost its sense of genuine education.   It is a re-enactment of the blind leading the blind (or as one wag put it, "the bland leading the bland").

(ii) It is to be questioned if university education is intended to produce the gentleman.   Is it not rather to produce the scholar?[23]   Certainly much of what we call scholar and what Newman calls gentleman overlap.   But is not "gentleman" more a word of society than of the university?   It is expected that every scholar be a gentleman.

(iii) The twentieth century has seen the failure of the scholar.

The German and Italian universities did not, as now the Russians do not, oppose the dictatorial rule placed upon them. Worse than this, some of the professors became active agents in dispensing poisonous propaganda.[24]   The profound belief of Renaissance man in the cultural and ennobling powers of education *per se* is found out to be too optimistic.   In view of these developments it is hard to resist the judgment that Newman read too much into the sheer ennobling power of liberal education itself.   It would be interesting to have Newman's assessment of Soviet education.   Would he not perhaps even deny it was education?

The Christian college, however, is at a point of advantage here, and is in agreement with Newman. It can produce the Christian gentleman.   In fact, it ought to produce the Christian

22. Cf. Gordon Clark, *A Christian Philosophy of Education,* and H. Zylstra, *A Testament of Vision.*

23. We do not mean the technical scholar but the person with scholarly standards, scholarly insights, scholarly abilities, and the maturity that education in scholarship brings.

24. It is interesting that the small but significant opposition to Hitler came more from a few pastors and theologians than from the scholars (as a class).   In the Church, however, the issue was complicated by the notion of obedience to powers that be.

gentleman. Because it is usually a small school, and because it can formulate a coherent theory of Christian education and implement this theory, the Christian college of today stands at a door of opportunity it has not had for many decades.[25]

(3) *A university is Christian when it is guided by the Church.*

That the Roman Catholic Church should actively enter into the academic life of a university is the most Catholic part of Newman's philosophy of education, yet the issue raised is relevant to any Protestant college or university. Any institution which bears a Christian charter must show its moral integrity by exhibiting a positive relationship between itself and its Church.

Newman has two fears about Roman Catholic university education. *First,* he fears that the Roman Catholics will be tempted to pull away from education and surrender university education to Protestants or to the state. But Newman will not allow this. Newman "was certain that the only way to meet modern intellectual infidelity was on its own grounds — through a courageous program of higher education."[26] *Second,* he fears that a Catholic university would get out of hand and cease to be a truly Catholic university. The only answer to the second fear is a set of ground rules which will protect the freedom necessary for scholarship and yet permit supervision by the Roman Catholic Church.

Newman did not view the active participation of the Roman Catholic Church in the life of the university as the brazen intervention of an ecclesiastical institution in the life of an academic one. The philosophy behind this is the belief that truth is arrived at corporately rather than individually. According to Roman Catholic opinion, the evil in Protestantism is *individualism.*[27] Individualism has no means of correcting erratic opinion. If each individual is a center of truth, then

25. See the stimulating article to this intent by Earl J. McGrath, "Let the Church College Be Itself," *The Christian Century,* 78:1459ff., December 6, 1961.
26. Harrold, *op. cit.,* p. 94.
27. Cf. R. S. Devane, *The Failure of Individualism.*

there are as many truths as there are individuals. Roman Catholicism believes that the endless divisions among Protestants are sufficient condemnation of individualism whether in scholarship or theology.

On the contrary, the Roman Catholic Church is an organism. It has lived through the centuries, carrying a common life and a common theology with it. It contains within itself a great diversity of personal and national differences and these are great corrective devices. In military language, it represents the staff concept of command in contrast to the command of one general. If the lone general is a Napoleon or a Hannibal, all goes well; but if he is incompetent, all is lost. The staff will work slower and less brilliantly, but in the long run it wins more battles than it loses.

Newman knew the temptations of a university. It is liable to convert the spirit of the liberal arts and the spirit of the educated gentleman into its philosophy of life, and so oppose the Christian revelation. Universities as well as persons may suffer from "individualism." And individualism means error, for it does not have the power of inner correction. Consequently, universities need the balancing force of the Roman Catholic Church as much as individuals do. Newman's thesis, accordingly, is that the Roman Catholic Church is necessary for the integrity of a university, for it steadies the university in the performance of its office.[28]

This does not mean merely that here and there the Church offers a steadying hand. It means much more. It means that the guidance of the Church pervades the life of the university. A theological faculty on the campus does not make the university Christian. That which makes a university Christian (and Catholic) is expressed in the following words of Newman.

> . . . A direct and active jurisdiction of the Church over [the university] and in it is necessary lest it should become a rival of the Church with the community at large in those theological matters which to the Church are exclusively com-

28. Cf. Newman, *op. cit.*, p. xxix.

mitted. .... And in like manner, it is no sufficient security for the Catholicity of a university even that the whole of Catholic theology be professed in it, unless the Church breathes her own pure and unearthly spirit into it, and fashions and moulds its organization, and watches over its teaching, and knits together its pupils, and superintends its action.[29]

In line with this strong statement is another equally strong one: "If the Catholic faith is true, a university cannot exist externally to the Catholic pale, for it cannot teach universal knowledge if it does not teach Catholic theology."[30]

Newman next explains concretely how the Roman Catholic Church can maintain the integrity of its university. In *science,* the scientific spirit might so grip the researchers that they first ignore and then forget the invisible. It is the function of the Church to remind them of the spiritual order.[31] In *literature,* the student certainly is exposed to the finest products of the human spirit. But, reasons Newman, "man will never continue in a mere state of innocence; he is sure to sin, and his literature will be the expression of his sin, and this whether he be heathen or Christian."[32] The man of letters can be carried away by the aesthetic qualities of literature and then the aesthetic spirit replaces the religious spirit. The Church must correct this. *Philosophy,* too, can go astray. Only under the direction of the Church may it reach perfection; if it goes its own way it falls into error. The irony here is that philosophy is supposed to be the pre-eminent cure of error.

It is a natural reaction of some Roman Catholics to retreat from literature, philosophy, and science, and so avoid these evils. Newman's mind is just the opposite. The Church is to correct the bad in university education and is to attempt to inspire her students and scholars to greater academic excellence. In one of Newman's finest pages he tells us that one of the functions of

29. *Ibid.,* pp. 186 and 187.
30. *Ibid.,* p. 186.
31. Cf. De Hovre, *op. cit.,* p. 309.
32. *Op. cit.,* p. 198.

the university is to prepare for life in the world.[33] It would be
a disservice for the university to give a protected education. The
only place to learn how to swim in troubled waters is in troubled
waters.   The Christian university must therefore *trouble* the
waters! If the university shields the student from all the hard
and the atheistic and the sinful opinions of the ungodly, it
will not really accomplish its intended goal. The student will
encounter them the first day he leaves the university. Let
the university be as rough as it can, for only in this manner
can it prepare students for a rough world. But let it be the
roughness of Christian hands.

The thesis of Newman that the Roman Catholic Church
should enter the life of the university in an active way immediately calls to the center the issue of academic freedom. How can
we reconcile an authoritarian Church with the free pursuit of
knowledge?

Newman handles this problem two ways: *first,* he appeals
to the harmony of truth. The truth of God in Scripture, in
nature, in the Church, and in the study is one truth and if one
truth, one part cannot contradict another part. But in the ac-
quisition of truth many tensions, difficulties and problems most
certainly arise. No scientist or scholar would think of junking
the pursuit of knowledge because this situation prevails. Harder
work and more diligent research is demanded and eventually the
contradiction is resolved.

Similarly, if some scholar should come to the conclusion that
his research led him to a point of conflict with theology, he
should not therewith be through with theology. But as it is
customary in patient scholarship, he should exercise forbearance
and work towards a resolution of the conflict, and this may not
come in his lifetime.

Second, controversial matters should be kept to the scholars.
Newman recognizes that scholarship needs elbow room. The
Catholic university must grant this room. But new ideas are

33. *Ibid.,* p. 202.

not to be indiscriminately spread.[34]   They are to be restricted
to scholarly societies and scholarly journals.   In this way the
scholar has his academic freedom and the Catholic layman is not
disturbed by a new theory which may or may not eventually
prove itself.

Newman certainly touched on delicate issues in the philosophy
of a Christian university, namely, the relationship of the university to the Christian Church and the status of academic
freedom within a "committed" university.   Both of these problems have been difficult ones in the history of American
Christian colleges.   In the next lecture we shall touch upon a
creative philosophy which attempts to resolve these tensions.

34. Unfortunately Newman sides against Galileo. *Ibid.*, pp. 191 and 223.

Lecture IV

ABRAHAM KUYPER (1837-1920):
THE SACRED SECULAR

I. The Man

Abraham Kuyper was a man full of life. He found every aspect of life exciting, and he lived each day to its fullest. Twice he poured out his energies so completely that he suffered physical collapse. Whatever he did, he did with fullness of vitality, with superhuman dedication, and with marked ability. Not many men end their lives as Kuyper did, with eight decades of dramatic, interesting, exciting and rewarding life behind them.

As a preacher he was energetic, forceful and eloquent. He never wanted for hearers. As an orator he was one of Holland's finest. His speeches before the legislative bodies of the Netherlands leave no doubt about that. As a theologian, he was considered by some as the finest Calvinistic theologian since the Geneva master himself. Kuyper was also a man of letters. The amount of written material he produced is immense. The critical bibliography of his writings takes three volumes. He was constantly writing lectures, special addresses, political speeches, pamphlets or books. For most of his adult life he edited and wrote for two journals, *De Standaard* (*The Standard*) and *De Heraut* (*The Herald*). His enemies feared his pen and feared his oratory. He was recognized by the journalists of Holland as one of their finest, and the editor of the leading Catholic journal thought he was *the* finest.

Kuyper was as much a politician as he was a theologian. From the age of thirty-six until the day of his death he was in politics.

For many years he was a representative, for four years a prime minister, and always the leader and brightest star of the Anti-Revolutionary Party. He once said that fear of politics "is not Calvinistic, is not Christian, is not ethical."[1]

As an educator he was almost without peer. When a child, he exhibited an enormous hunger for facts. In the university he won a gold medal for a prize essay. This essay as well as his doctoral dissertation was written in Latin. He not only wrote Latin but spoke it fluently. He thought Latin should be mastered because it was not only the language of theology, but also the most excellent language for training the mind. He also studied Hebrew, Aramaic, and Arabic among the ancient languages. In the early days of the Free University he taught Hebrew. He was fluent in the modern languages of French, German and English.

He was university founder, rector, professor, author of texts, and educational statesman. The leading spirit in the founding of the Free University of Amsterdam, he was rector of it from time to time. There he taught theology, Hebrew, homiletics, aesthetics, and Netherlands language and literature.

His appetite for knowledge was never satisfied. A river of books and journals flowed into his study. He never talked with a person (whether of high or low status) without learning from that person all he could of his craft. As a result, in many ways he was ahead of his times. When Holland was plagued with great strikes during Kuyper's political career he suggested labor legislation, which was outrageous to his contemporaries, but very wise in the light of later labor developments. He also is the one man to whom technological education in the Netherlands owes the most. He sensed the coming of a great technological age (as Newman did not) and as prime minister enacted legislation to strengthen the technological education of the country.

Kuyper was an impressive teacher. No student went through

1. Frank vanden Berg, *Abraham Kuyper*, p. 53.

his lectures unmoved. More than once he became so enthusiastic about his subject that the lecture merged into a profound devotional hour. The students were continually overpowered with the range of his learning. One of their games was to try to "stick" him with questions of historical detail to see how expertly he knew dates and sequences of events.

He gave much in lecturing, and expected much from the students. He considered the opportunity to study a gift of God's grace, and therefore those who were given the gift should not look down upon those who had not received it. The motivation to study should be the highest. Kuyper thought learning for personal gain unethical. He had little patience with laziness and demanded hard, consistent work. As a Christian, the student's first task was to find the *Logos* in creation, and in all his studies he must ever be close to God.

III. THE SITUATION

In 1799, a young German theologian published a work which is customarily taken as the beginning of a movement known as German rationalism or neo-Protestantism or modernism or liberalism. The man was Friedrich Schleiermacher, and the book was *Religion, Speeches to Its Cultured Despisers*. By the time Kuyper became a university student at Leiden, this movement had captured the theological faculties of the three Dutch universities. One of Kuyper's professors was Keunen, famous for the Graf-Wellhausen-Keunen critical theory of the composition of the Old Testament. Another was Scholten, who was a brilliant lecturer and scholar, and a remarkable personality. Under the influence of these men, especially Scholten, Kuyper embraced the liberalism of the time. When Scholten announced from the lecture platform that he no longer accepted the bodily resurrection of Christ, Kuyper was among the students who applauded.[2]

Later on, Kuyper was won back to the orthodoxy of his home

2. *Ibid.,* p. 23.

and youth through the consistent testimony of the orthodox folk in his first pastorate. Kuyper ministered to both the liberal and orthodox members of his congregation, and the contrast was remarkable. In fact, it was so decisive that he was won back to orthodoxy when he saw that the orthodox members of his congregation believed something, knew why they believed it, and lived stalwart lives consistent with their beliefs.

In contrast to its professed "liberalism," liberalism was really narrow and intolerant and gave no quarter to that segment of the Church which remained loyal to the confessional standards. Doctrinally, it had become so radical that it permitted baptism in faith, hope, and charity rather than in the name of the Father, Son, and Spirit.

Theological education was in the hands of this liberal element. Consequently, there was considerable unrest over theological education and occasionally meetings were held to protest it. But nothing concrete was done about it. Kuyper, too, was concerned with this impasse in theological education. He diagnosed it as incurable. The law of the land was such that legislative correction seemed impossible; the spirit of the liberals was such that there was no hope of their changing their course of action; and the universities themselves did not wish to change it. The theological faculty of the University of Amsterdam had gone so far as to turn the Old Testament lectures over to a Jewish scholar.

Kuyper and his friends became persuaded that the only remedy was a new university, a free university built upon a very different concept. Within the continental structure of university education, the new concept was a radical departure from the pattern of centuries' duration. Beginning with the medieval period, the state, the Church, and the universities formed "inter-locking corporations." Universities were state controlled and state financed, and their theological faculties educated for the Christian ministry. Furthermore, only those schools which were within this structure could grant degrees. To suggest a university not governed by the state and not supported by the state, its theologi-

cal faculty not the pawn of either Church or state, was therefore
a most radical suggestion.

Kuyper and his friends could have settled for less. They
could have founded a seminary solely for the training of ministers
loyal to the historic confessions of the Reformed Church of Holland. But Kuyper would not hear of this.

First, a lasting movement cannot be built upon a superficial
foundation. An enduring Christian witness cannot be built
upon a remarkable personality, a theological journal, a religious
paper, or a society for the promotion of truth. An enduring
movement must be institutional, and only a university could pro-
vide the stability for a great cause.

Second, the Church is a society within society. It has the
responsibility of the perpetuation of its own ministry. But, being
a society, it also has a cultural life, and this calls for scholars,
lawyers, doctors, authors, and theologians. Otherwise, the Church
bears only a partial witness in its society. To have an institute
or a seminary in which only ministers are trained and the rest
of professional life is untouched would be like furnishing an army
with only one kind of weapon and expecting it to take successful-
ly to the field. The cannon is useless for close combat and the
rifle is useless against the strong fortifications. The Church
needs the products of an entire university, not only the products
of the institute or seminary. The separation of the doctrine of
the Holy Spirit from the progress of science is not Reformed
faith but Anabaptism.[3]

We cannot take the space here to tell again the remarkable
story of the founding of the Free University. It has been told
for us in some detail in the biographies of Vanden Berg and
Kolfhaus. Under fierce criticism and amidst bitter feelings, the
university opened its doors with five professors and five students.
In those difficult years Kuyper refused to be discouraged, because
for a Calvinist discouragement is sin.[4] Eventually the school

3. Cf. Wilhelm Kolfhaus, *Dr. Abraham Kuyper, 1837-1920, Ein
Lebensbericht,* p. 155.
4. *Ibid.,* p. 159.

did come to an hour of triumph. As prime minister, Kuyper had legislation enacted which reconstructed the university and technological education of Holland. One of the provisions of this legislation was to grant full academic status to free institutions which were academically worthy. This included (at the time the only such institution) Kuyper's beloved Free University of Amsterdam.

III. THE UNIVERSITY

Newman and Kuyper had one trait in common: they did everything from principle. Both reflected about university education in terms of principles. But there is also one great difference between the two men. Newman complained that he had neither the gifts nor the temperament to be an administrator, and this was one reason his attempt to found an Irish Catholic university failed.[5] On the contrary, Kuyper was highly gifted in forming plans and in executing them. He was not only expert in theory, but also had remarkable powers of leadership. His distinguished political life crowned by his four years as prime minister is sufficient witness to this. Kuyper saw his dreams materialize, and the institution he guided into existence still exists today in Amsterdam.

The following principles, in my opinion, are the major ones which entered into Kuyper's philosophy of Christian higher education:

(1) *A Christian university is justified by the Christian doctrine of creation.* The center of the Christian faith is the person of Christ, the redemption He accomplished, and the salvation He bestows. But, being so preoccupied with Christ and redemption, we can readily become victims of "funnel vision." Kuyper had his faults but funnel vision was not one of them. He saw that many Christians were so preoccupied with the Chris-

---

5. "Neither by my habits of life nor by vigour of age, am I fitted for the task of authority or of rule, or of initiation." *On the Scope and Nature of University Education,* p. 207.

tian doctrine of redemption that they had lost sight of the great doctrine of creation. Kuyper argues in many places in his writings that we must take our fundamental stance on the doctrine of creation. It is in the doctrine of creation that we see the original purposes of God for man. Man was created to be *lord* of the natural order, to *found* a society, to *create* a culture within this society, and to *understand* creation. God did not create a man, or solitary individuals, but a humanity. And the concept of humanity is organic, social, and cultural. The vision of a paradise as an effortless existence in tropical abundance is just the opposite of Kuyper's notion of paradise. To him paradise (if continued) would have been a beehive of activity, with man industriously carrying out the great intentions of his Creator for him.

In short, the original creative purposes of man were: (i) to worship and serve his Creator: (ii) to create a humanity through reproduction; (iii) to form a society and its culture; and (iv) to be the lord of the universe in the twofold action of mastering it and understanding it. We see at this point a principle of Kuyper's not really understood by Augustine, Melanchthon, and Newman as it relates to education. Kuyper takes in stride the problem that stumped Newman (science, technology).

Kuyper knows that sin has worked its terrible effect in man, society, and the cosmos. But the entrance of sin did not negate the original purpose of God for man in His creation.[6] Man is still called to dominion over creation; he is still under the ordinances of creation; art is still a function of the power of imagination divinely given at creation; and science is but one of the ways man exercises the dominion given to him at creation. Sin has changed much, but it has not changed these purposes of man which derive from creation.

Kuyper vigorously opposed any attempt to cut man into two parts, nature and grace. He equally opposed any attempt to

6. Abraham Kuyper, *Calvinism*, p. 92.

build a wall between the world of the redeemed and the world of society. He was firmly convinced that we have to do with one humanity and one world. He did not think that the doctrine of sin overpowered the doctrine of creation. Consequently, he was a vitriolic critic of the Anabaptists, for they represented this unholy dicing up of man and the world. For example, he wrote that "the avoidance of the world has never been the Calvinistic mark, but the shibboleth of the Anabaptists."[7]

Man as sinner is still God's creature. Man as redeemed is still a child of creation. We cannot deny creation in order to glorify redemption. Human depravity must not obscure the ordinances of God still binding upon sinful man. We must not emphasize the eternal man and lose sight of the temporal man, nor must we deny the earthly in man through an undue emphasis upon the heavenly.[8] We must not disrupt nature in order to magnify grace. We cannot preoccupy ourselves with the spiritual to the neglect of the bodily and temporal. We cannot be so concerned with Christ the Redeemer that we forget God the Creator. We must not have so narrow a view of Christ as personal Saviour that we lose sight of His cosmological significance. To emphasize this, Kuyper wrote:

> It is not true that there are two worlds, a bad one and a good, which are fitted into each other. It is one and the same person whom God created perfect and who afterwards fell, and became a sinner — and it's this same "ego" of the old sinner who is born again, and who enters into eternal life. So, also, it is the one and same world which once exhibited all the glory of Paradise, which was afterwards smitten with the curse, and which, since the Fall, is upheld by common grace; which has now been redeemed and saved by Christ, in its center, and which shall pass through the horror of the judgment into the state of glory. For this very reason the Calvinist cannot shut himself up in his church and abandon the world to its fate. He feels, rather, his high calling to push the development of this world to an ever higher state, and to do this in constant accordance with

7. *Ibid.*, p. 72.
8. *Ibid.*, p. 118.

> God's ordinance, for the sake of God, upholding, in the midst
> of so much painful corruption, everything that is honorable,
> lovely and of good report among men.[9]

Human nature in sin is still a nature created by God; the
universe under a curse yet abides as God's handiwork; society
in corruption is still God's society; and culture, wayward and
sinful, still bears the marks of God's original intention. Therefore the Calvinist must be more world-affirming than world-
denying, for otherwise he betrays the Christian doctrine of
creation. *Kuyper vigorously defends the sacredness of the
secular.* He was not blind, however, to the necessity of some
world-denying. He says that Calvinists have been opposed to
dancing, card-playing, and theater-going on the grounds that
these modes of entertainment compromise the moral seriousness
of life. Although these three items have been the subject of
petty comment from the pulpit and worldly-wise lampooning by
other Christians, Kuyper's discussion is marked by authentic
moral dignity and principle.[10]

Kuyper's point of leverage in teaching a world-affirming faith
is his doctrine of common grace. The terms "general revelation"
and "special revelation" are common in contemporary theological
discussion. General revelation is a revelation potentially common
to all men and reflected in creation, providence, and the nature
of man. Special revelation is God's special, saving word known
only by Christians in faith and through the Holy Spirit. Kuyper
makes a similar distinction, the seeds of which are found in
Calvin, in his doctrine of grace. God's special grace is His
redemptive grace through Christ; God's common grace is His
mercy turned towards all men. If the course of sin were un-
checked, it would totally corrupt the race. But if it is to be
checked, it can only be checked by grace. But not all restraint
of sin is the operation of saving grace. Hence that grace which
checks sin but does not save is *common* grace (*algemene
genade*). It is common or general in that it operates on all men.

9. *Ibid.*, p. 73.
10. *Ibid.*, pp. 73ff.

Common grace is God's grace which so retards sin and so strengthens man's powers that he is able to carry out to some degree of success the original creation purposes of God.[11]

Common grace deters. It prevents sin from working its terrible and final effect upon man and society. It is a restraint upon the individual man, keeping him from the full range of deeds of depravity, and upon society, preventing it from total moral corruption. Common grace relaxes the curse.[12] It so modulates God's wrath that man has the space, time and freedom to develop the resources he was endowed with at creation. It provides a common basis for the co-operation of believer and unbeliever in the common pursuits of life.[13] It is the source of moral good in the unregenerate as well as of the true, the beautiful, and the good in his culture. It is the ground and the preservative of the family, of the state, of science, and of education. It is the basis of the Christian concern for art, culture, and civilization and the condemnation of all those Christians who wish to flee the world (*der Weltflucht*). Common grace represents the continuation of the rule of God in the world and therefore does not permit the Christian on principle to isolate himself from the world. It is the reason why Christians ought to honor science among unbelievers, to see the gift of God in the unregenerate, to esteem a Socrates, a Plato, or an Aristotle.[14] Common grace is a mandate to Christians to commit themselves to the common cultural tasks of their society. It was out of this strong conviction that Kuyper wrote the following:

> A Calvinist who seeks God, does not for a moment think of limiting himself to theology and contemplation, leaving the

11. In passing, it is to be noted that the common idea that Calvin taught a total corruption of man and the race is far from the truth. Calvin and Calvinism have taught the total *inability* of man to redeem himself, but they have never taught that man and the race have reached maximum corruption.

12. *Ibid.*, p. 30.

13. *Principles of Sacred Theology*, p. 158.

14. Cf. *Calvinism*, p. 121, and Kolfhaus, *op. cit.*, p. 192.

other sciences, as of a lower character, in the hands of unbelievers; but on the contrary, looking upon it as his task
to know God in *all* his works, he is conscious of having been
called to fathom with all the energy of his intellect, things
terrestrial as well as things *celestial;* to open to view both
the order of creation, and the "common grace" of the God
he adores, in nature and its wondrous character, in the production of human industry, in the life of mankind, in sociology
and in the history of the human race. Thus you perceive
how this dogma of "common grace" suddenly removed the
interdict, under which secular life had lain bound, even at
the peril of coming very near a reaction in favor of a one-
sided love for these secular studies.[15]

The doctrine of common grace enables the Christian to
appreciate art, culture, and education without for one minute
obscuring his doctrine of sin. It enables him to proclaim the
goodness of the world and yet not mix the rule of Christ with
the dominion of sin. It enables him to honor the gifts of God
in the sinner without honoring the sinner. It enables him to use
the world with all that was wrought into it by God at creation
without contaminating himself with the depravity of man in
the world.

In Kuyper's great treatise *The Work of the Holy Spirit,* he
develops this in terms of his doctrine of the Holy Spirit. All
gifts of men come from God. Calvin had argued this in the
early chapters of the *Institutes,* for to Calvin the gift implied the
Giver. Kuyper traces these gifts to the Holy Spirit. Therefore,
wherever there is the skilled laborer, the military genius, the
expert lawyer, the capable statesman, the great orator, the
able government official, there is the operation of the Holy
Spirit.[16] Kuyper also believed that every vocational gift is a
gift of the Holy Spirit, for the Holy Spirit lights up the personality, and gifts are elements of the personality. In *The Principles of Sacred Theology,* he taught that we must learn to

15. *Calvinism,* p. 125.   Italics are his.
16. *The Work of the Holy Spirit,* pp. 38-39.

recognize that science is a gift of the Holy Spirit.[17] Thus the universal or general action of the Holy Spirit is parallel to the doctrine of common grace, and together they bear their witness for the necessity of Christian participation in culture across its entire spectrum.

This rather long excursus, which seemed to have little to do with university education, was absolutely necessary. Kuyper proceeds from principle, and therefore university education must be grounded in sound theological thinking. And it has taken this much space to lay down this necessary theoretical foundation. The conclusion is ready to be drawn: a university is the most effective institution devised of men to perpetuate man's cultural life, his scientific life, and his theological life. It is grounded in the doctrine of creation and in the doctrine of common grace. It follows from the doctrine of creation, for it is man's concerted effort to create culture, perpetuate culture, and and through science be the lord and knower of the universe. It follows from the doctrine of common grace, for it is one of those institutions of men created and sustained for the good of the human race.

Therefore, only the Christian has the real justification for a university; and if Christians wish to participate in education they cannot be true to the doctrines of creation and of common grace unless they create nothing short of a university.

(2) *A Christian university must conform to the essence of a university.*

If a university is justified by the Christian doctrines of creation and common grace, it must be truly a university. A university has a certain character (recall Newman), and only the school which measures up to that character has the right to the title of a university. The justification for a university is not the justification for *any* university. Any Christian university must comply with the essence of a university, otherwise it is not truly

17. P. 192. Note how Kuyper makes a creative response to science. Augustine's Platonism prejudiced him, and Newman doesn't quite know how to manage this juggernaut.

a university, regardless of all its boasts to being Christian. According to Kuyper, there are two things which form the essence of a university, and any proposed Christian university must conform to these criteria.

(a) *A university must be a free corporation.* The university pursues knowledge or truth by means of scientific procedures. The word "science" is used here in its broader Dutch and German sense, not in the more restricted sense of the English language. But the pursuit of knowledge and truth by strict scientific procedures can occur *only in freedom.* Kuyper spells this freedom out in some detail.

First, there must be political freedom. A university in its essence is a free corporation. Any pressure or supervision destroys its essence. One source of such pressure is the state. Hence for a university to live in freedom, it must be free from pressure from the state. This idea of Kuyper was most revolutionary in view of the history of continental education. Kuyper had a great admiration for the American universities, for they came far closer to the ideal of a free corporation than continental state-dominated schools.

Kuyper rejected the notion of the omnicompetent state, or the all-powerful state. The state has authority in all territories of the culture, but it is not to be all-powerful in any of those territories. Its role is to supervise all territories and protect the rights proper to each territory. Thus the state sets up the academic standards for a university to protect the standards of education.[18] But beyond that it may not interfere with the internal life of the university. In its own sphere the university has the right to enjoy its own sovereignty.[19]

It is not difficult to imagine Kuyper's reaction to education con-

18. As Elton Trueblood observes, it is *standards* which make education education. He has a sharp page on the inflation of honorary degrees in America, and particularly the excessive granting of the doctor of divinity degree. "The greater number of honorary degrees that are given, the cheaper they become." *The Idea of a College,* p. 180.

19. Kolfhaus, *op. cit.,* pp. 163-164.

trolled by the state, whether in Fascism, Nazism, or Communism. For him, the purpose of education is not political. Education is a matter of culture, a matter of the general health of a society, a matter for the development of humanity. To make a university political destroys the essence of a university. There is no omniscience in politicians which enables them to determine truth; truth is determined by the principles of scientific investigation; and such investigation can be true to itself only in an atmosphere of political freedom. The university must be free to formulate its own curriculum, free to hire its professors, and free to govern its own internal life.

Second, there must be freedom from the Church. That the Christian university should be free from the Church sounds radical. But this assertion reveals part of the greatness of Kuyper. He certainly was one of the greatest defenders of orthodox Christianity and historic Calvinism in his generation (along with James Orr of Scotland and B. B. Warfield of America). But he was convinced that if the essence of a university is the scientific pursuit of truth, then any pressure corrupts this pursuit, even pressure from the Church. Kuyper went further. Even the theological faculty is not one upon which the Church may rightfully exert pressure. Although the theological faculty does educate for the ministry, it has also the responsibility of pure research in theology. If the Church is constantly "riding herd" on the theological faculty, it prevents the faculty from conforming to the rules necessary for the pursuit of truth. The Church is not to be the trustee of the theological faculty to insure its orthodoxy. Much more important than officious supervision is the prevalence of a spirit of heartfelt mutual trust between Church and theological faculty.[20]

The Church must not bring pressure to bear upon the faculty of the university. Even if the Church must suffer, it must keep its hands off and let science be sovereign in its own territory. There is no question that science can go astray, but a Church

20. *Ibid.*, p. 156fn.

that is strong will not fear the possible aberrations of learning. The Church must simply recognize the essence of a university. The prophets were free men; the Greek schools were free schools; the earliest Christian schools were free schools; and the great medieval universities were originally free schools. When the papacy realized what a "plum" it had in the universities, it exerted its influence upon them, and at this point the universities compromised and lost much of their freedom. The Reformation revived the ideal of the university as a free corporation. To mix Church and education is to mix things which do not belong together. Therefore in order to preserve the integrity of the Christian university it must be free from state and Church and be sovereign in its own sphere.

Third, there must be academic freedom. There is a frequent confusion of the right of free speech (political) with academic freedom (scientific). Academic freedom is the sovereignty of the university in its pursuit of truth. It means freedom in research, freedom in lecturing, freedom for publication, and freedom for the pupils to learn. To be free *for* the truth, the university must be free *from* pressures from both Church and state. This is the real meaning of academic freedom, and it is freedom for professors (*Lehrfreiheit*) and for students (*Lernfreiheit*). And a Christian university must have academic freedom if it is to conform to the essence of a university. We note in passing how much more creative and academically sound Kuyper's thought about academic freedom is in contrast to Newman's *ad hoc* solution.

Academic freedom is one of the more difficult problems of a Christian school and Kuyper devotes much space to it. The Christian commitment to revelation seems to exclude a robust practice of academic freedom. How do we reconcile the *finality* of Christian revelation with the *openness* of academic learning?[21]

21. Cf. *Principles of Sacred Theology*, pp. 171ff., and *Calvinism*, pp. 126ff. Cf. also Alfred De Quervain," Die akademische Lehrfreiheit als theologisches Problem" (*Theologische Studien*, Heft 25) ; Georg Froher,

Objection 1: "Theology cannot be a science because it is bound to the content of revelation and therefore represents a *closed* matter."

Answer: It is true that theology is bound to revelation, but this is no more than saying that science is bound to nature. If revelation were a mere listing of prescripts and theology but the reading off of these prescripts, then theology would be bound by revelation. But if the Scriptures have a historical and literary character, there is full freedom granted to the scholar in determining the meaning of the revelation. Thus theology meets the criterion of academic freedom at this point.

Objection 2: "Theology can progress only as the Church gives its consent and therefore theology cannot be truly scientific."

Answer: Certainly the Church, to be the Church *in essence*, must come to her convictions about truth. We simply cannot deny this to the Church without denying the very meaning of the Church. But the Church only wishes to say something firm about *saving faith* (i.e., about those doctrines which actually *form* the Church), and what is outside this boundary is certainly open territory for the scholars.

When the Church, however, does say something about saving faith, it does not issue a purely authoritarian pronouncement. What it says was determined through conflict of opinion and argued within the full rights of academic freedom. Both sides, or all sides, have had their say and the matter is determined out of this churchly debate. Granted, a situation may arise in which the scholar and the Church disagree. The scholar then has the moral and academic obligation to show the Church that he is right. If the Church dissents, then the scholar must leave the Church. But the theologian does not lose membership in the society of scientific theologians because he offers a dissenting theory, for the Church is not a scientific academy. It

"Das Problem von Lehrfreiheit und dogmatischer Bindung in der evangelischen Theologie und Kirche," *Theologische Zeitschrift*, 13:260-284, Juli-August, 1957; and the *Monthly Staff Report* for February, 1960, of The American Association of Theological Schools.

is at this juncture that Kuyper wrote the following remarkable lines:

> Hence in the realm of [the new birth] one remains a man of science, even though he may lose harmony with the church of his birth; and it is not science, but honesty and the sense of morality, which in such a case compels a man to break with his church.[22]

Objection 3: "In that the results of theology are determined in advance, how can theologians be true to the pursuit of knowledge?"

Answer: The assumption made here is only partially true. The theologian is limited to the authority of Scripture; even so the scientist is limited to the deliveries of nature. If theology is thinking God's thoughts after Him in Scripture, science is thinking God's thoughts after Him in nature. But the details are as open to the theologian as they are to the scientist. And "if a conflict arises between the result of our investigation and our ecclesiastical creed, it may render our ecclesiastical position untenable, but it cannot affect the maintenance of our scientific results."[23]

In a second discussion of academic freedom Kuyper begins by affirming that "to accomplish this task, scientific theology must be entirely free in her movements."[24] Although this discussion and the previous one are about the freedom of the theologian, what is said pertains to all the faculties in a Christian university. The first point he makes is a repetition of his previous discussion, namely, that the scientist is as much bound to nature as the theologian is to Scripture. His second observation is that there is a difference in the arrangement between a pastor and a Church, and that between a professor and a university. There are certain terms in the arrangement which, if violated, end the arrangement. But the arrangement has nothing to do formally with academic liberty. That is, the arrange-

22. *Principles of Sacred Theology*, p. 173.
23. *Ibid.*, p. 174.
24. *Ibid.*, p. 593.

ment (or contract) speaks only of the internal life of the Church or university, not of the universal pursuit of truth. If a Church finds that the pastor violates the terms of the arrangement, then it has the right to dismiss him; if a university finds a professor violating the terms of his contract, then it has the right to dismiss him. For example, if the professor of theology in a Lutheran faculty should defend Roman Catholic dogma the curators of the university have the right to dismiss him. "Yea, stronger still, a theologian who, in such a case, does not withdraw, is dishonest, and as such cannot be upheld."[25] But theology is still a science and canceling the right to teach in a given university is not the denial of the right of the dismissed professor to pursue his theological studies. In short, either the Church or the university has the right to enforce terms of a contract or arrangement, but not to prohibit the right to pursue truth.

If the theologian is to pursue the truth, he needs freedom. He must not be under pressure from the Church to call white black. Even though some theologians are superficial or arrogant, their freedom as scholars must be respected. The Church must go one step further, therefore, and allow the professor to publish his conclusions. Even if these views go contrary to the Church, the Church must permit it.

But on the other hand, the theologian must be a man of *courage* and *honesty*. He must be willing to publish his views whatever the personal sacrifice may be, for only in this way is the truth fully served. But he must also be a man of marked honesty, and when he sees that his views transgress the confessional limits of his Church he ought in all honor to withdraw.

To use an analogy, says Kuyper, the truth of God is not given

25. *Ibid.,* p. 594. The unlovely specter of the authoritarian Church or ecclesiastical official or "important pastor" throwing his weight around in the internal life of a Christian school is well known. Equally disastrous, equally unlovely, but seldom highlighted is the dishonest professor who teaches with tongue-in-cheek while basically violating the terms of his arrangement. Kuyper is very right in asserting that the academic freedom granted the professor *must be matched by the professor with scrupulous honesty.*

to the Church as sliced bread, but as wheat. There is the necessary milling process between the wheat and the bread. So God's truth is given to us as wheat and not as bread, i.e., as a list of propositions or theses. In the milling, refining, and baking of the wheat of revelation by the theologian, liberty must be granted. Consequently, the Church, in good theological principle, must grant academic liberty to her theologians.

Certainly the diversity among theologians is shameful, or embarrassing or regrettable to some. Not so to Kuyper. There is progress in any science, theology included, only if there is friction and ferment. If this friction and ferment is eliminated, then the possibility for scholarly greatness is eliminated. "Liberty is for genuine science what the air we breath is for us."[26] There can be no monarchs in a university. Error and truth cannot be judged by an ecclesiastical court; only in honest conflict can truth and error be judged.

The Roman Catholic Church has been in great error here. First, she corrupted the meaning of the doctor's degree by sponsoring universities. The degree is not an honor bestowed by the Church,[27] but it possesses the dignity bestowed upon it by the scientific character of a university. Secondly, when a scholar under the supervision of the Roman Catholic Church arrived at a position contrary to the supervising Church, he either had his scholarly wings clipped or his neck wrung.[28] Nor did the Roman Catholic Church anticipate the great future of science, and the struggles that must involve the scientists if the truth is to be pounded out to a conclusion.

(b) *A Christian university must be a complete university.* Kuyper would not settle for a theological seminary to correct the Church condition in Holland. His concept of creation and cul-

26. *Calvinism*, p. 126.
27. Kuyper is not speaking here of the honorary divinity degree; his point is that a university is not a university in virtue of a papal charter, but because it is a scientific institution.
28. *Calvnism*, *p.* 128. This is one aspect of the history of higher education Newman did not do justice to.

ture precluded that short-cut solution. Only a university can fulfill the needs of the Church and of the state. But this university must be a complete university. Consequently, Kuyper argued for the five faculties of the Dutch university (Theology, Philosophy, Medicine, Philology or Literature, Jurisprudence). These five faculties are not arbitrary but reflect a grounding in the nature of things. Each faculty corresponds to a fundamental relationship which man sustains to himself, to his culture, or to his universe.[29]

In full agreement with Newman, and for the same reason, Kuyper argues for the inclusion of theology as the fifth faculty. This he supports on two grounds: (i) if any faculty is admitted into the curriculum because it represents one of man's fundamental relationships, then theology must be admitted because it represents the most fundamental of all relationships, man's relationship to God. (ii) The second reason is that theology is knowledge, i.e., it is a science. And if knowledge, it belongs to that institution whose business is knowledge, namely, a university.[30]

In summary, a Christian university has the right to the title only as it conforms to the essence of a university by being, first, a free corporation and, second, a full university of five faculties.

29. Kuyper's philosophy of the university curriculum is argued in *Principles of Sacred Theology*, pp. 211ff.

30. Kuyper was far more aware of the structure of Christian knowledge than Newman. For example, judging from contemporary philosophy of analysis, Kuyper had a much deeper grasp of the special character of theological assertions than Newman. The details are spelled out in *Principles of Sacred Theology*. Furthermore, for Kuyper religion or the science of religion was no substitute for theology. For him, the fatal mistake of modernism was to substitute the science of religion for the science of God. Kuyper did once dream the dream of modernism (Vanden Berg, *op. cit.*, p. 24), but renounced it and spent the rest of his life combating it. Thus the typical "broad-minded" department of religion in a typical university does not, according to Kuyper, really know what it is talking about. At this point Kuyper and Barth would agree. The study of religious phenomena (psychological, historical, or sociological) is not the same as theology, the science of God.

(3) *A Christian university must be permeated with a consistent Christian world-view or life-system.*

Kuyper and his friends could have founded a university on a broad orthodox platform that would admit many different viewpoints among its faculty members. It could have been a rallying point for Methodists, Lutherans, and Baptists too. But, according to Kuyper, this is sending a boy to do a man's job. The Christian faith is caught up in a great conflict. One army pushing towards it is religious liberalism, which threatens the life of the Church. Another is the spirit of the new science and the new scientific philosophy. Yet another is the strife of Christianity with the great non-Christian religions. No leveled-out interpretation of Christianity (no matter how orthodox or fundamental) is adequate for the kind of warfare required. Only a consistent world-view or life-system of Christianity will do, and to Kuyper this meant the full Reformed faith, or Calvinism.

A university is the center of such a battle because that is the place where principle confronts principle. Each of the enemies of the truth of God is itself a life-system, and can only be combated with a life-system. Anything short of a Christian life-system will not do. No list of fundamental doctrines will do. To start a Christian university around a minimal creed is unrealistic, in view of the greatness of the battle. Therefore, a Christian university must be founded upon a Christian life-system, and to Kuyper this meant Calvinism.

At this point we must not prejudge the issue by some stereotyped understanding of Calvinism. To most people, Calvinism means total depravity, election, and predestination. It meant this to Kuyper too, but he saw these doctrines as special applications of larger principles. He saw Calvinism as a world-view, as a life-system, as a comprehensive perspective from which one looked upon science, art, politics, philosophy, psychology, and economics. It was this kind of Christian world-view and this kind alone which would be adequate to the demands put upon it in the rough and tough exchange of academic life.

Kuyper was no bigoted Calvinist. He knew that faith was wider than creed. He had a great admiration for D. L. Moody in his evangelistic crusades in England. He was ready to recognize faith in Jesus Christ wherever he saw it, and he could sing and pray with Christians everywhere who honored the name of Christ.[31] But for the battles of academic life, only a consistent Calvinism was adequate. Those people who boasted that they could write the gospel on a postcard thought they were emphasizing the simplicity of the gospel, but in reality were confessing their poverty in understanding the Christian faith.

Kuyper is very contemporary in his opinion that all thinking is *from* presuppositions. There can be no thinking without presuppositions and therefore all respectable thinking is from sound presuppositions. Any "neutrality" in science, philosophy or religion is fictional. The only respectable procedure is to admit that one thinks from presuppositions and to choose those presuppositions in a responsible manner. Kuyper chooses Calvinism as containing the best presuppositions for the guidance of life and for the Christian university.

Calvinism must not be interpreted as one scheme of salvation among many. It is that, but it is something more. It was Calvin who saw the cosmic dimensions of the Christian gospel, and therefore saw it as wide as creation, as expansive as culture, and as comprehensive as man's total social life. This principle in essence is "in the widest sense cosmological, the *Sovereignty of the Triune God over the whole cosmos,* in all its spheres and kingdoms, visible and invisible."[32] And in virtue of this Kuyper bore his testimony in the following: "In Calvinism, my heart has found rest. From Calvinism have I drawn the inspiration firmly and resolutely to take my stand in the thick of this great conflict of principles."[33]

To Kuyper, thus, Calvinism is a total life-system. It is a form of religion, fosters a specific kind of religious consciousness,

31. Cf. Kolfhaus, *op. cit.,* p. 160.
32. *Calvinism,* p. 79.   Italics are his.
33. *Ibid.,* p. 12.

defends a particular kind of theology, offers a special Church order, inspires a political and social philosophy, defends a moral order, sets forth the proper relation of nature and grace. It relates the Christian to the world, has its own doctrine of Church and state, and forms the proper basis for the appreciation of the arts and sciences.[34] Therefore, a Christian university will be great only as it sails under the banner of a full-orbed Calvinism.

Kuyper, however, was no repristinationist or reactionary. He did not long for the good old days. He had too much power of life and breadth of understanding to want to recreate Geneva. He said emphatically: "We are no miniatures of Calvin, but fruits of his spirit."[35] Calvinism must be kept up to date if it is to be adequate to the conflict. In fact, so strong was Kuyper in making Calvinism contemporary that he was accused of doctoring Calvin for his own purposes. But he was resolutely opposed to the petrifying (*Versteinerung*) of Calvinism. The Reformed faith must always be reforming. The confessions of past centuries must be rewritten so that they will speak to the present century.

It is this fresh, vigorous, cultural, and comprehensive Calvinism which is, for Kuyper, to form the presuppositions of a Christian university. It is a life-system to be taken with great courage and frankness. It intends that Jesus Christ shall be king of every subject matter. It sees things as God sees them, which is as He has revealed them in His Word. From this God-given perspective, it sees the total individual life, social life, Church life, and political life. It confesses that the foolishness of the cross is not something we sermonize about; it is something which is poured into our blood.

Calvinism is not meant solely for the theological faculty but is the presupposition for every faculty of the university. The Christian medical faculty, for example, does not look on a sick

34. *Ibid.*, p. 17.
35. Cited by Kolfhaus, *op. cit.*, p. 178.

man as a sick animal, but as a creature in the image of God. The Christian medical professor does not tell his students to keep people uninformed of impending death, for man must face this as a spiritual as well as a biological crisis. The Christian professor sees the Christian principle in jurisprudence, in science, in language, in history, in philosophy, and in world history.[36] "Upon the heritage of our human lives there is not a strip an inch wide exempt from the call of Christ: 'It is mine.' "[37]

Kuyper knows that Christianity has always been in conflict. The conflict is raging and will rage. It is ultimately a conflict of two principles, an anthropocentric or a theocentric, the word of man or the Word of God, human wisdom or divine revelation. This conflict rages in the university, and the Christian educator ought not to ignore it or play it down or to attempt to circumvent it. The anthropocentric principle must be met head-on with the Calvinistic principle. Nothing short of comprehensive Calvinism will do. It is no use trying to save the upper stories if the first floor is on fire. Therefore, the Christian university must be built upon a powerful Christian life-system, a coherent, comprehensive and consistent world-view.

This great conflict reaches its maximum intensity in a university. Therefore the Christian university must diagnose the conflict, ascertain the Christian stance, and then govern its entire life from that stance. Then it will truly be a Christian university in substance as well as in name.[38]

36. Kolfhaus, op. cit., pp. 167ff.
37. Cited by Kolfhaus, op. cit., p. 169.
38. Kuyper did not believe in two kinds of truth, two kinds of science, but two kinds of men (normal and abnormal, Christian and sinner, regenerate and unregenerate), and two kinds of principles (theocentric and anthropocentric). Truth is one, so the conflict is not in truth but in men and in their divers principles. Cf. Calvinism, pp. 131ff., and Principles of Sacred Theology, pp. 106ff.

Lecture V

SIR WALTER MOBERLY (1881-   ):
REDBRICK VERSUS OXBRIDGE

I. The Twentieth Century

Redbrick stands for the new industrial and technological universities of England, and Oxbridge for the great classical tradition of Oxford and Cambridge. The new spirit in education began in the middle decade of the last century, and we saw the conflicts it engendered reflected in the writings of Newman. We also saw how Kuyper tried to encompass it within his broad Christian world-view.

The British academic landscape is now dotted with the Redbrick universities, and the Oxford and Cambridge of Newman's academic days have forever disappeared. A number of very able educators even believe that the very concept of a university has been hopelessly corrupted or destroyed, and that the modern university is no longer really a university.[1] If England has the Redbrick university, America has the Drive-In state university, or Occupational college. And both of these function on a mass scale, with the universities swallowing freshmen by the thousands on registration week and regurgitating them back into society four years later.

Like all institutions of higher learning the Christian college was caught in this revolution from Oxbridge to Redbrick. It was also caught in the theological revolution of religious modernism. Some schools became so modern in educational philosophy that they became secular and lost all meaningful Christian

1. Cf., for example, R. M. Hutchins, *The Higher Learning in America.*

witness.   Others pulled back, and, while preserving a Christian witness, became third- and fourth-rate academic institutions.

The nineteenth century saw the alliance of the Christian college with theological liberalism as well as Christian humanism.   The uniform result was the loss of an authentically Christian witness.   A number of colleges became secular; others became nebulously Christian under the title of "Church-related colleges" — a term which Trueblood for good reason deplores.[2]

Seeing this, or anticipating it, some colleges attempted to preserve the evangelical faith through a strong and censorious administration and a weak and restricted scholarship.

It is within the context of these two revolutions that Sir Walter Moberly wrote *The Crisis in the University* (1949). This man and his work commend themselves to any discussion of the Christian college in the twentieth century, for Sir Walter writes as a Christian;[3] he has been in the center of British university education. He has, for example, been chairman of the very important University Grants Commission; and he has attempted to create a philosophy of higher Christian education relevant to the university situation in the twentieth century.

In using Moberly, however, we must do some transposing of thought.   Moberly writes for the British situation, and it differs markedly from ours.   Because there is an established Church in England and none in America, some of his discussion does not apply to us.   We must engage in the risky business of reinterpreting Moberly for the American scene.   Calculating from what he says of British education, we shall attempt to frame what he would say for an American Christian college.

II. Moberly's Principles of Christian Higher Education

(1) *A Christian college, to perform its task properly in the twentieth century, must thoroughly acquaint itself with the*

2. *The Idea of a College*, p. 16.
3. Cf. pp. 8 and 25 of *The Crisis in the University*.

historical, cultural, and educational factors of modern higher education.

It is Moberly's contention that we cannot understand our present situation until we have acquired a proper historical perspective. The Christian college must be critically self-conscious of the traditions of university education. Accordingly, Moberly gives an analysis of the three basic traditions in university education.

(a) *The Christian-Hellenic.* This is the Oxbridge (Oxford, Cambridge) tradition, enshrined in Newman's great work *The Idea of a University.* Moberly lists five characteristics of education in this tradition. (i) It is liberal education in that it cultivates the intellect; it is not training in skills but the formation of the person. (ii) It is general rather than technical education; it seeks the enlargement of the mind, whereas specialization so canalizes the mind that the mind does not truly become educated. (iii) It is systematic education, and not merely the wholesale storing up of unrelated facts in the memory cells of the brain; it believes more in thoughtful digestion of important materials than in the accumulation of vast piles of information. (iv) It is education that arises in a community of learning, a community of professors and students, where the fatherly concern of the professor is matched by the filial regard of the student. (v) It is Christian education in that the Christian faith is given a respectable place in the curriculum of the school, and in that the Christian faith exercises a pervasive influence in the thought-life of the university and in its devotional life.

(b) *The Liberal (or German Scientific).* In this tradition education has the following characteristics. (i) It is more concerned with investigation than with instruction, with the advancement of science than with the communication of knowledge; faculty members are experts in knowledge rather than masters in lecturing. (ii) It is learning for learning's sake, leading to detailed knowledge and technical scholarship. (iii) Education is conducted in separation from the state, the Church, commerce, and industry. (iv) Education is — or is supposed to be — free from presuppositions. (v) Education is detached from that which activates men's emotions — be it state, or Church, or politics. (vi) Education is conducted according to the highest possible standards and within a community of intellectually superior people, professors and students. (vii) Education is conducted with maximum freedom for the faculty in regard to what they are to teach, and how, and when. (viii) Education is conducted with maximum freedom for the student in regard to what subjects he is to take, how he is to study, and how he is to behave.[4]

(c) *The Technological and Democratic.* This is the tradition of the Redbrick university of England, the Drive-In university of America. According to it education has the following characteristics.[5] (i) It is empirical, relying heavily upon the scientific method. (ii) It is analytic, emphasizing dissection into components rather than creative synthesis. (iii) It is activistic, practical, and utilitarian, viewing the measurable, weighable, and manipulatable as more valuable than the unseen or intangible.

In the beginning of his third chapter, Moberly mentions a fourth tradition or period, *The Chaotic.* The Christian-Hellenic and the Liberal German (or scientific) have been replaced by the Technical-Democratic, and the latter has degenerated into the contemporary Chaotic.[6] The Christian educator must understand this exactly if he is going to guide his own school with wisdom. What does Moberly mean by the Chaotic? He means that the goals of university education have become so diverse and ambiguous that our universities are universities in name only, not in essence.

4. Cf. F. Paulsen, *The German Universities,* "Lernfreiheit," pp. 201-211.
5. This was the tradition forming in the days of Newman, that which he branded as education for utility. Kuyper saw it coming, but instead of denying it he attempted to call it into Christian service through the Christian doctrines of creation and common grace.
6. *The Crisis in the University,* pp. 50ff.

Suppose we make a list of the factors which have historically made a school a university — and not a trade school, or a professional school, or an occupational school, or a political indoctrination center, and the like. Then let us check out Redbrick University and Drive-In University according to this list. The disheartening result is that both universities fail to comply with the list. For example, historically a university is supposed to produce the well-rounded person. Redbrick and Drive-In turn out the narrow specialist. A university education is supposed to create a truly cultured intellect in the student (so expertly spelled out by Newman). Redbrick and Drive-In graduate students whose only interest is utilitarian or vocational and therefore essentially selfish. A good university education aims to create minds that are truly objective and genuinely critical. But Redbrick and Drive-In turn out graduates who are burdened with all kinds of uncriticized presuppositions.[7] A university is supposed to be a "university," a corporation, a guild of professors and a guild of students, in short, an academic community with no dilution of the communion in community. Redbrick and Drive-In, to the contrary, look more like a bargain sale or an academic cafeteria. *Thus, judged by the traditional and historical criteria of the essence of a university, neither Redbrick or Drive-In are a university. They are, in fact, Chaotic.*[8]

The next question Moberly explores is why Redbrick and Drive-In have become Chaotic University. He lists five factors: (i) Such universities do not treat fundamental issues; rather, they are concerned primarily with the learning of details. The

7. Gordon Clark put his finger on it when he wrote that "a narrow technical training provides no safe-guard against being deceived. Only a liberal arts education that uncovers three thousand years of human motives, foibles, reflections, and devices offers hope." *A Christian Philosophy of Education*, p. 25.

8. Of course a student can obtain a classical education (using the term widely) in Chaotic University. To deny this would deny too much. But the point of Moberly, Clark, *et al.*, is that Chaotic University will graduate a student *without* his having achieved the essentials of that education which truly is *university* education.

expert in French literature can drown his class with his immense treasury of details but never pauses to tell the students why Pascal should be prefered to Voltaire, or Fénélon to Talleyrand. (ii) Such universities are characterized by a false neutrality. Both Newman and Kuyper saw this. In religion, ethics and politics, the university is supposedly neutral, but neutrality on such issues is always a vote for evil. Political neutralism was Hitler's strong ally; ethical neutralism leads to amoralism; and religious neutrality is no less a commitment to atheism than faith in Christ is commitment to Christianity. Such universities are fragmentized. Instead of being a coherent whole, the university is split into various technological institutes or elite trade schools, and the students come to the "university" to get training for an occupation. (iv) Such universities carry on their life in a context of uncriticized presuppositions. To have presuppositions is not wrong, but to be unaware of them is. (v) Finally, such universities dodge the ethical and spiritual factors of education. An educated person should be able to make responsible decisions; but when a university gives no moral or spiritual education, the graduate is not educated to make responsible decisions.

Although Moberly's attack on Redbrick University is one of the sharpest in our century,[9] it is not the only one. There is general unrest over university education. We have seen the beginnings of this unrest in Newman, who prophetically saw the end of real university education if it yielded to the standard of "utility." One of the latest blasts comes from A. Whitney Griswold, president of Yale University, who labels the modern university a "service-station" university.[10]

9. "Britons have decided that it [*The Crisis in the University*] is one of the most thoughtful, responsible critiques of the British university since John Henry Newman's *Idea of a University*." *Time*, LIV (July 11, 1949), 77.

10. *The University* (The Fund for the Republic, Inc., 1961). In his comment at the conclusion of the pamphlet R. M. Hutchins notes that Michigan State University now offers a degree with a major in Mobile Homes! "As Mobile Homes come in, civilization goes out" (p. 27).

With attacks on contemporary universities come also the remedies. Moberly discusses three proposed remedies and finds each failing to be remedies despite whatever virtues they might have. A Christian College which is acting responsibly will make itself knowledgeable about currently proposed remedies.

(a) The first remedy is *scientific humanism*. This is the remedy offered by scholars who believe in the omnicompetence of the scientific method. It is the heart and soul of the Communist higher educational system in particular. According to this philosophy of university education, the university exists for political reasons, namely, to serve the state. The universities are encompassed in the total planning strategy of the state. The function of the university is to supply the educational needs of the state, *as these are determined by the state*. Universities are to forward the welfare of the total population instead of promoting the stability of a class within society. The universities are also to be bearers of the culture of the modern state, the specific kind of culture proper to a scientifically-minded society.

The chaos in our universities would end if the state stepped in and reorganized the universities and made them effective institutions for the state. The university will not be a place of impartial or neutral or objective scholarship, but it will serve the body politic just as *all* institutions of the state do. Its spirit will be the spirit of scientific rationalism, its concrete goal the education of technical personnel for the state, and its ultimate goal the forwarding of social justice for the masses.

Although Moberly rejects this philosophy of education as the solution to chaotic university education, he pauses long enough to learn from it: (i) Scientific humanists have seen through our uncriticized presuppositions; (ii) they have seen the necessity of linking education vitally with contemporary culture; and (iii) they exhibit a passionate concern for human welfare. On the debit side of this theory, however, even more may be said. The demand for practical results will drive out those intellectual values — values in themselves as Newman so rightly said — which are part of the very *being* or *essence* of a university. And so Moberly writes the following biting sentence: "To equate our awed hush of wonder in presence of a great poem or picture or symphony with our enjoyment of a crossword puzzle, shows an odd insensitiveness to values."[11] Moreover, the university is not an institute or an occupational training center or an advanced "how-to-fix-it" shop. Its heartbeat is theoretical thought, and when practical demands stifle theoretical activity the university begins to die.

And, it should be noted well, practical considerations themselves suffer, for in reality the theoretical precedes the practical.[12]

Just as academically wicked as driving the theoretical off the campus is the subjection of the life of the university to the

11. *Op. cit.*, p. 74.
12. *Ibid.*, p. 74. Professor Gerhard Ebeling of Zurich has a telling comment to the same point. He is writing specifically about the temptation to delete all theoretical concern from theological education for a totally practical education. But what he says applies to all faculties. Ebeling's style is complex but his meaning can be grasped. "Nothing is said against concern with more or less one-sided, specialized questions of theological science which grow out of the internal considerations of the substance of theology, and which involve a dimming of one's headlights towards the present times. To the contrary, the ability to do such specialization, the endless patience in preoccupation with the non-actual, the readiness to entertain surprising discoveries against all models and standards of the present, is directly the presupposition for a factual procedure in the chief problems of theology. Meanwhile, the narrow-minded, short-circuited hunt after the directly actual and the practical and useful is the death of responsible theology. It stands to reason that a man can achieve success in theology only in working with a burning question of the times through the strong education of scientific schooling in the classical theological disciplines. The weakening and repressing through well-intended but unreflective proposals for the reform of studies in favor of an amateurism [*eines Diletterens*] would achieve in all other possible specialized studies [i.e., physics, biology, etc.] exactly the opposite goal from the proposed intentions." Ebeling thus says that it takes a person with a thorough *theoretical* training to handle competently a *practical* question. The really serious, concrete, practical yet complex and difficult problem is beyond the competence of the person whose education is solely pragmatic or practical. "Hauptproblem der protestantische Theologie in der Gegenwart," *Zeitschrift für Theologie und Kirche*, LVIII (April, 1961), 131.

state. Here we remind ourselves of Kuyper's distinction between the sovereign right of the state over all the territories within it so as to protect their rights, and the sovereign rights of these territories within themselves. The very nature of a university demands that it be sovereign within its own realm. It cannot become the instrument of Church, state, or industry without its essence being corrupted. The crime which the Nazi regime committed against the German universities was not only that it used the universities as tools in its own cause, but that it used the universities as tools of the state at all. "To be clay for human potters is a degraded form of being."[13]

The final criticism by Moberly of the university of scientific humanism is that it is based upon an erroneous world-view, and by its very nature this world-view will be reflected in significant aspects of the university's life.

(b) The second proposed remedy is *classical humanism,* a proposed solution made famous in America by R. M. Hutchins and in England by Gilbert Murray, one of the finest Greek scholars of our generation. The philosophy of education of this theory for recreating the true university is composed of the following theses: (i) The supreme aim of education is to teach the art of living. The true, the beautiful, and the good are the objective criteria of the good life; these are free from personal or racial idiosyncrasies. If a university does not teach the art of living, it becomes a trade school which teaches the art of making money, or it becomes a pawn of the state (as in the Russian system), or it becomes a revival center for edification (as in many schools influenced by the Puritan tradition). (ii) The good life has been structured for us by the Greeks, and progress is but filling in the outline. The Christian theological virtues presuppose the Greek natural virtues, so that Christian and secular education can unite at the ground floor of the natural values. (iii) The good life recognizes a hierarchy of values, and therefore our universities must teach *discrimination.*

13. Moberly, *op. cit.,* p. 78.

The student must know on what grounds the symphony is of more worth than the circus, or the good novel than the football game. This leads to a refinement of taste, which is one of the major criteria for differentiating the educated person from the merely trained person. (iv) Finally, the classical tradition is built upon the objective. The proposed return to classical humanism is to be undertaken not for sentimental reasons but for substantial reasons. The modern scientific gains are not to be written off, but on the other hand without the values of the classical tradition education in science does not really educate.

It is surprising that Moberly finds the scientific humanistic university more commendable than the classical humanistic. After a brief commendation of classical-humanism, he launches a sharp refutation: (i) This approach represents a dated outlook. It can be held only by a very few persons who romantically interpret the past. It is plainly not relevant to an urbanized, industrialized, and commercialized society. This possibility Newman failed to reckon with adequately; Kuyper did, however, in his reconstruction of the technological education of Holland and in the place he gave to science in his philosophy of education. (ii) It is naïve. The rough, brutal and anxiety ridden history of two wars makes this approach look very much out of touch with the world as it is in the twentieth century. Something "at once more realistic and more dynamic is needed."[14] (iii) It is myopic. It fails to see the inevitability of change and the values in change. Parallel to this, it fails to grasp how conditioned our life is. Thus classicism can never really responsibly keep up with the ever-moving shoreline of cultural change. (iv) It is provincial. It has little room for natural science and underrates its significance. True, it admits science to the university and it learns the theories of science, but it

14. *Ibid.*, p. 97. One must be careful at this point not to identify "classical education" with "liberal arts education." One may with Moberly disagree with a return to the classics and yet maintain a strong belief in the place of liberal arts in education.

remains impervious to any real contribution from science. (v)
Finally, it is class-structured. Classical humanistic education is
really education for a privileged stratum in society. As Harrold
remarks, Newman's gentleman was "the financially independent
and well-bred man of leisure . . . who had little premonition
of the demands of science and technology as we now know
them."[15]   But, continues Moberly, the modern world with its
social, economic and political revolutions cannot tolerate a
university built upon the Victorian ideal of a gentleman.

(c) The third proposed remedy for the chaos in university
education is *Christianity*. This was suggested by a report in
1941 issued by the Archbishops of Canterbury, York, and
Wales and bearing the title, *Christian Education: A Call to
Action*. The logic behind the proposal is as follows: (i) The
most fundamental relationship of man is his relationship to
God, and a disturbance of this relationship disturbs *all* of life.
Unless academic healing begins with this relationship we will
be treating symptoms and not diseases.   (ii) Our universities
are ships without rudders, and the only rudder worth having
is that of Christianity. Back, then, to the original Christian
foundations of Oxbridge. Back to Newman! Back to Thomas!

Again Moberly surprises us. He is a dedicated Christian
man and we might expect him to defend vigorously this
philosophy of education, but he backs away from it. We must,
however, keep in mind the British situation, which does not
parallel our own situation, and remember that Moberly is not
speaking of the Christian college as we know it. But what he
says at this point is eminently worth-while. His objections to
Christianizing the universities are the following.

(i) It is impracticable. The modern university has departed
from the Christian synthesis of the medieval university and it
is not possible to return to the cultural climate of the thirteenth
century. (ii) It is inequitable. It would be imposing upon the
majority, composed of non-Christians, the will of the Christian

15. *John Henry Newman,* p. 92.

minority. Moreover, this could be done only with heavy-handed politics which no Christian could stomach. (iii) It would be a delusion. We would not be imposing authentic Christianity upon the university but at best some sort of compromise religion, a dilute religion. At best it might be a broad theism with a few moral principles. But, as Moberly incisively argues, Christianity is Incarnation, Redemption, and Resurrection[16] and we cannot be Christian and sacrifice these. At this point Moberly is most refreshing in contrast to so much uncritical pap one reads about "religion on the campus." (iv) The final objection is that the Christianizing of university education might be very harmful for the course of scholarship. It would definitely be a strong damper upon opposition to accepted Christian positions. But the history of the university and of culture has shown that in many instances the critic has been right and the Church wrong. The Christians no more possess infallible truth than the non-Christian lives in total error. If university life is dominated by the theologians, the creative and fruitful role of criticism will be cut off, and what our universities would gain in Christian conformity they would lose in scholarly greatness.

(2) *A Christian college of the twentieth century must have an actively Christian faculty.*

Having made itself familiar with the complexities of university education in the twentieth century, the Christian college must now attempt to pick out a realistic course of action. Moberly is very clear in insisting that *since we cannot remake the cultural patterns of the twentieth century, we had best adjust our philosophy of Christian higher education so as to live more effectively in the conditions of the twentieth century.*

Moberly believes that the real clue to the problem lies with the individual faculty member. There is a crucial task that the faculty member can perform that neither the administration nor the supporting Church can. In a word, Moberly's most

16. *Op. cit.,* p. 103.

important thesis is that authentic higher Christian education depends upon the perceptive, learned, informed, dedicated Christian professor.

Again and again Moberly slashes out at the intellectually non-committed faculty member. The real threat on the faculty is not the atheist, the Communist or the naturalist. It is the non-committed intellectual. His radical disease of non-commitment shows that he has not been educated, and the persistence of non-commitment into this stage of his life shows that he is *uneducable*. When this non-committed person is a Christian professor the error and evil are compounded with interest. Such a person never correlates his Christian faith and his academic life. Moberly puts it this strongly: "A Christian who draws no guidance for academic policy from his faith is failing in his duty as a member of the university community; he is also failing in his integrity as a Christian."[17] *If the faculty is not Christian in a deeply committed sense, then there is little hope in maintaining a Christian college.* Moberly's program as applied to the Christian college is the program of making the faculty thoroughly Christian.

(i) *Every faculty member must be a lay theologian.* If a faculty member is to be an effective and responsible witness to the Christian faith, he must have more than an amateur's knowledge of that faith. He must apply some of his academic competence to Christian theology and become a good lay theologian. Moberly's four standards for a good lay theologian are: first, he must be able to read his Bible intelligently; second, he must have an understanding of Christian doctrine commensurate with his own academic ability; third, he must know the world situation and how to interpret it from a Christian perspective; and fourth, he must see the correlation between his specialty and the Christian faith.

This last point is aimed at the professor who perfectly compartmentalizes his faith and his specialty. Take, for example,

17. *Ibid.*, p. 27. Cf. pp. 261ff.

the psychologist who attends morning worship on Sunday and thinks that he has thereby fulfilled his Christian obligations. On Monday morning he is "pure" psychologist. His reading, lecturing, thinking and research are set for him exclusively and exhaustively by the science of psychology. He never attempts to find out what Paul, Augustine, Thomas, Luther, Calvin, Pascal, or Kierkegaard might contribute to an understanding of man. He may even teach a Sunday-school class and give his class a good lesson each Sunday; but on Monday he never asks himself what is the bearing of the Christian doctrine of creation, or sin, or the Holy Spirit, or the Incarnation on his understanding of man.

(ii) *Every faculty member must become a vital, dedicated Christian.* The modern secular spirit, to which the Christian college is not immune, has a way of crowding out spiritual life, of dampening Christian zeal and discouraging theological seriousness. Christian professors must make a special effort to overcome this deadening influence, and to maintain a vital personal faith, and to deepen theological comprehension.

The dedicated Christian professor believes that only in Christianity is there a solid basis for education. He believes that only the Christian world-view can truly integrate the currently disintegrated state of knowledge. The alternatives are as both Newman and Kuyper put them: a Christian life-system or a man-made life system. He knows that the latter will be defended by able men and scholarly men. *Even so, he does not shy away from the sharp edge of decision but reckons that this decision is one of the most vital elements of the Christian faith.*

This decision must be re-enforced by life as well as by doctrine. It must be sustained by a daily life of sincere Christian piety. Or put otherwise, a man's experience of the God in Jesus Christ must be as profound and meaningful as his dedication to Christian truth. Or, as Kuyper put it, we must always be near God in our studies.

(iii) *Every faculty member must bear his witness in his academic life.* Moberly is writing of the British situation, where many faculty members of Redbrick are also Christians. The retreat of these faculty members into theological anonymity is, he believes, most regrettable. The *first* need of a university, a strong Christian witness, is the *last* thing most professors give. But if there is to be healing in our universities some of it must come from dedicated Christian professors.

Moberly thinks that the notion of a neutral university is false,[18] and that the squeamishness about religion in our universities is deleterious. The Christian religion has been the religion of the Western world. The Christian Church is the birthplace of the university. The culture we live in is a culture permeated with Christian principles. What justification is there for excluding from our campuses one of the greatest cultural heritages of Western nations? And what justification has a Christian professor for a retreat into anonymity in his academic life?[19]

Moberly thinks that the Christian professor ought to bear his Christian witness before other faculty members, before the students, and in his administrative work. Otherwise by his very silence the Christian professor continues the disintegration of our universities. But this witnessing must be done in wisdom. The professor must know the difference between witnessing and propaganda. It must be a dignified, honest, "nonthreatening" witness comportable with an academic community.

Although Moberly is speaking of the Christian professor in the state school, his remarks also apply to the professor in the

18. Cf. the three incisive chapters on neutrality in education in Clark, *op. cit.,* Chapters IV, V, VI.

19. One such professor confessed that if he were not religiously anonymous it would cost him his advancement or even his job. Evidently it is glorious to be eaten by lions, but only humiliating to suffer for Christ's sake in a university. We suggest to every such timid university professor that he read Otto Dibelius's great sermon on cowardice, "Against Cowardice," *Christianity Today,* VI (Jan. 19, 1962), 356-359.

Christian college. One can retreat into spiritual and theological anonymity there too!

(iv) *Every faculty member must recognize the limits of his situation.* A university is not a church.[20] Therefore Christian professors must realize that they are in a university. The first temptation of the Christian professor is to protect students from harsh views towards Christianity. The Christian professor is a pastor to students, but he cannot protect them. Moberly is one with Newman on this point. One learns to swim in troubled waters only in troubled waters. If a student cannot stand jostling around, critical attacks, or bold denunciations of the Christian faith, we are not to silence the professor. Rather, we are to send the student home. A Christian student who cannot take the rough and tumble intellectual life of a university does not belong there. This is quite a different philosophy than that of the over-solicitous pastors who want a Christian education taught with kid gloves.

The atmosphere of university life must be open. It must allow for sharp disagreements among the faculty, and freedom for divergent opinions. Moberly argues this not on academic grounds, but on theological grounds. Christians can, because of their own sinfulness, talk themselves into believing that they have the final truth on certain matters. If the atmosphere in a Christian college becomes that of a closed corporation, then there is no possibility of a corrective — a point Melanchthon made against the scholastics. But if there is a measure of non-conformity allowed on the faculty, this will keep the Christian college from prematurely closing in on the truth.

But there is yet another reason. The Christian is to respect all opinions in a university because these opinions are offered by individuals. As Christians it is part of our ethic to respect individuals. Just as the Christian knows that no group is wise enough to be free from error, by the same token no opinion

20. A point already made by Kuyper and also by Douglas Eadie in his address, *Religion on the Campus* (1961).

offered in a university is bad enough to be overlooked. There-fore, Christian professors ought not attempt to censor their colleagues.

(3) *A Christian college of the twentieth century must have an expert faculty of theology.*

Moberly gives a brief history of the status of the faculty of theology in a university. In the earliest universities theology monopolized the curriculum. Everything was taught for its ecclesiastical and theological service. In the second period theology had a place of primacy, expressed in the saying that theology was the queen of the sciences. This was the mature university of the Middle Ages. In the third period theology held a place of equality with the other faculties. This was the situation in Oxford and Cambridge at the end of the nineteenth century. Finally, the theological faculty is barely tolerated. This is the present situation in the British universities and in many church-related colleges.

Moberly deplores the present situation. He believes that theological faculties should be equal in every way with the other faculties. We would add that in a Christian college the theological faculty should be the finest, in virtue of its great responsibilities. Moberly tells us what these responsibilities are.[21]

(i) A theological faculty has the responsibility of advancing sacred learning. The members of this faculty have as their special task the systematic investigation of the Christian faith, and to this task they must bring a scholarship second to none among the faculties.

---

21. It is to Moberly's credit that he does not give us a dilute notion of theology such as that given by the psychology of religion, or the sociology of religion, or the history of religion. Rather, "theology *is* the study of the self-revelation of the living God" (*op. cit.,* p. 282, italics are his). The basic premise of theology is that God has spoken to Israel through the prophets, to the Church through His Son. If this were not the case, there could be no theology. Furthermore, the theologian must himself be a man of great personal piety, for the separation of theology from spiritual life is wicked.

(ii) A theological faculty has a responsibility of preparing for the Christian ministry. Moberly does not mean that the college competes with the seminary, but rather that the Christian college is to give an adequate preparation for the professional training. How does a Christian college do this? It does it by getting the ministerial student into the thick of things. It does it by breaking up ministerial or theological or ecclesiastical cliques on the campus, for these represent or symbolize retreat from life. University days are days when the mind must be exposed to all sorts of old and new, radical and conservative, familiar and strange viewpoints. The cloistered cliques of the campus must not prevent this. If these cliques are allowed, the students are thus permitted to harm themselves, for in retreating from life they weaken their ability to serve God and the Church in their later life.

(iii) A theological faculty is responsible to the other faculties of the college. A theological faculty must not form a clique within a college and so live an isolated existence. To the contrary, of all the faculties it has the chance of being the catalyst faculty. It is the faculty which can take the lead in conversation with other faculties. It can attempt, for example, to show the uncriticized presuppositions in one of the other disciplines, which the specialist himself often cannot see. Further, the theological faculty can well be the evangelist to the rest of the faculties, showing them that only in the decision of faith is the resolution of life to be found.

(iv) A theological faculty is responsible to the entire student body.[22] Students come to college with a juvenile understanding of the Christian faith. And in college they will hear and read much that is contrary to the Christian faith. Not every page of Church history, for example, is glorious. Christian man has many times soiled his hands, even bloodied his hands,

---

22. In his "Stanford Plan," Miller attempted to keep the Christian courses in the total life of the school by refusing to coop them up in a department of religion and by making them inter-departmental offerings. *Op. cit.*, pp. 131ff.

in the course of the centuries. There must be some rough sessions about the Christian faith in the department of philosophy or psychology. But this is the hour for the theological faculty! It can sponsor lectures on the Christian faith tailored for the instruction and edification of the entire student body.

As we put Moberly down, we cannot help but reflect upon the virtues of his book. First, Moberly is healthily realistic. He knows full well that any effort to turn the clock back, to retreat, to seek a solution of other centuries, simply will not do. Secondly, he has a very sensible approach to Christian problems. He knows that evading issues and over-protecting Christian students will not do. Thirdly, he is a dedicated Christian. He has rightly emphasized these two points: unless we have an intelligent and alert Christian faculty, we do not really have Christian higher education; and unless we have a sound, historical theology of Incarnation, Cross, and Resurrection, we do not really have the Christian religion or a Christian institution.

SUMMARY STATEMENT

Having surveyed the educational opinions of five famous men we are now in a position to sum up the meaning of their theories for the American Christian university (in which we also include the college).

(1) *A university is Christian only as it is Christian throughout.*

Augustine recognized this when he taught that the Christian must be the critic as well as the user of secular learning. Melanchthon attempted to lay the foundations of a university system that would be not only educationally sound but also thoroughly Christian. Newman taught that theology must be honored and used in all the faculties of a university. Kuyper saw the heartbeat of a university in a consistent Calvinism intelligently applied within every faculty. Moberly argues in the same vein when he demands dedicated Christians in every department of a university.

In the structure of the American Christian university this means that board, administration, and faculty must be composed of vitally Christian men. This is a hard and narrow road, but it is the only one. Any other policy leads to dilution and with dilution defeat of the Christian aims of the university. Furthermore, this requires a very clear, intelligent and biblical definition of *Christian*. We can make the term so broad that it becomes meaningless and so narrow that we cut off as possible choices for board, administration, and faculty many men who are dedicated Christians.

We repeat, the way here proposed is a narrow and hard road. The foe that is always around the corner is dilution. Some of our largest private universities were once warmly evangelical; now they are virtually secular. Somewhere in their history they began a series of small but fateful compromises which eventually led to the complete dilution of their Christian character. The only vestige of their original charter is an effete department of religion. Other schools have attempted a synthesis of religious liberalism and liberal arts education. But this has hardly produced vigorous Christian institutions. The product has been some form of dilute Christian humanism.

The board of trustees must be composed of Christian men because the master policies for the school are determined by it, and because it hires the administrative personnel of the university. Furthermore, when strategic policy decisions are to be umpired, it is the board which calls the play.

The administration must be composed of Christian men because the day-by-day life of the school is managed by the administration and it has a large hand in the hiring of faculty personnel. At many points the administration is confronted with the making of decisions, and these decisions must be distinctively Christian. If the administration fails in its Christian witness and Christian interpretation of education the Christian character of the university is doomed.

One of the most important functions of the administration is to hire new faculty members. Exactly at this point the dilution may well begin because appointments are frequently made under great pressures. There is the pressure of the empty post which must be filled in order for classes to have instruction; and there is the pressure from the academic side. A dean or a department head may feel a real need to strengthen the academic stature of a department. Under such pressures fateful decisions may be made. There is no ready-made solution to this problem but there must be a well-formulated plan of hiring which keeps Christian concerns central. Sometimes it is better to face the embarrassment of lack of staff than to hire at the expense of Christian considerations.

The faculty must be composed of Christian men because it has direct and daily touch with the student body and therefore has the greatest possible influence upon it for the Christian faith. The first requirement of a faculty member is that he be

Christian throughout in his daily life, that he maintain a quiet Christian stance in his classroom, in his academic community, and in his local community. The second requirement is that he know how to correlate his specialty with the Christian faith. This is a very delicate matter. He must not dilute the substance of his courses by forever making it so much grist for his apologetic mill. And when he engages in apologetics he must beware of sentimentalizing the faith.

In the Christian university the faculty of religion should possess the highest competency possible. It cannot evade competition and comparison. If the members of the department of religion are uniformly much lower in academic ability than members of other departments, then the Christian faith will suffer on the campus of the university, even though the other departments are Christian in staff membership and education. We agree with Moberly that the department of religion ought to be the finest on the campus.

(2) *A Christian university has the liberal arts at the center of its curriculum.*

We do not, of course, equate the liberal arts with a return to the classics. Too much has been accomplished in post-classical times in history, fine arts, philosophy, and literature for us to do that. When Augustine argued for the retaining of classical learning he was in principle arguing for the centrality of the liberal arts. Although Melanchthon argued directly for the classics themselves, in principle he was arguing for liberal arts. Kuyper's emphasis on philology, on Dutch literature, and on a full university of five faculties is also an argument for the worth of the liberal arts. Moberly's attack upon the vocational university, the drive-in university, the chaotic university, is an oblique argument for the abiding worth of the liberal arts, even though he did attack the proposed return to the classics.

There are several reasons why liberal arts must remain at the center of any university and therefore at the center of a Christian university. First, liberal arts education produces the cultured person. The cultured person knows the history of culture. He knows the continuity of the present with the past. He therefore understands, comprehends, sees through the culture in which he lives. He can interpret it to himself and to his students. Second, liberal arts education educates taste and the sense of values. In the study of civilization, art, philosophy, and literature the liberally educated man reflects upon the greatest products of the human spirit. He is able to discriminate between poetry and doggerel, between ballet and twist, between opera and third-rate musical comedy. Third, liberal arts education introduces the student into the theoretical foundations of knowledge and culture, and the geography of human knowledge. The liberally educated man knows the degrees of precision obtainable within the various sciences and disciplines; he knows the limits of literature, chemistry, and astronomy, as well as knowing the powers of each. Fourth, liberal arts education exposes the student to the great options — in literature, in philosophy, in philosophy of history, in theory of art, in politics, in economics. He is not the pawn of his upbringing or his prejudices.

Restricted training in the sciences, in engineering, in business, and the like, does not accomplish these four things. Therefore people with such a narrow or specialized education are hardly truly educated. There simply is nothing that educates like the liberal arts; and if this is the case, then a Christian university must have liberal arts at the center of its curriculum.

There is, however, another facet to liberal arts education in a Christian university. It is the foundation for theological scholarship. A liberal arts education produces the scholar, and the theologian therefore needs to be educated in the liberal arts.

Bible Institutes emphasize the Bible and doctrinal rectitude. But Bible Institutes do not turn out expert exegetes or great theologians. The very simple reason is that where there is no education in depth there can be no academic greatness. The Church has to look to university men for her great exegetes and great theologians.

(3) *A Christian university, within the common grace of God, shares in the transmission of culture.*

Augustine did not reject the profane learning of his times; rather, he saw the truth in it as the truth of God illegally held. Melanchthon, Newman, and Kuyper concur in believing that one of the purposes of the Christian university is to transmit culture. It was particularly Kuyper and Melanchthon who believed that the Church owed society this service. It was Kuyper who brought this service under the notion of the common grace of God; and it was Kuyper who said that no better institution than a university has been devised to date to do this service.

This means that the task of a Christian university must not be viewed too soteriologically. The base of the university must be as broad as the creative-redemptive base of Sacred Scripture. This means it must be concerned with the purposes of God in creation as well as in redemption. If it restricts itself to redemption, it will devolve into an academic revival center and lose any sense of responsibility to the general welfare of humanity. It may also become a "preacher-mill" and give the impression that the only worthy vocation is the ministerial vocation.

The creation of man was also the creation of a humanity. A humanity implies the existence of a social order and a commonwealth, both of which are under the creative will of God. Although sin fractured the creative purposes of God, it did not cancel them. Man is still to marry, beget children, and have dominion over the world. And this dominion extends over sociological, political, and scientific matters. In short, a humanity means a civilization under God. This civilization is possible only as culture is transmitted, and one of the more important means of transmitting culture is through the university. Therefore if the Church enters university education it must also grant this function of the university. In theological language, a Christian university must fulfill the creation orders of God as well as the redemptive orders.

This means that the Christian university educates for society as well as for the Church. In fact, most of its graduates will be laymen, and if the Christian university fulfills its task it will graduate informed Christian laymen. It will graduate Christian lawyers, Christian doctors, Christian engineers, Christian teachers, and the like, who will see their life-function as not only the bearing of witness to the grace of God in the structure of their calling, but as the fulfilling of the creative will of God in the welfare of the human race.

(4) *A Christian university relates itself vitally to the Christian Church.*

Although Augustine founded no university, he made his residence at Hippo a place for the training of men for the Christian ministry. He made a valiant attempt to bring together Church and education. A similar spirit breathed in Melanchthon, who wanted his universities to be great Christian institutions. Newman with his Catholicism is the most obvious advocate of an alliance between Church and university. Kuyper recognized the same problem that Newman saw but had a different interpretation of academic freedom. Thus Kuyper saw a mutual partnership of Church and university.

Jesus Christ founded no university but He did found a Church. Christianity can exist without schools, but it cannot exist without the Church. The Church is, so to speak, the mother of the university, not the university the mother of the Church. Therefore a university to be thoroughly Christian must maintain a *vital* relationship with the Christian Church.

This vital relationship is ambiguous in America because there is no uniform relationship of university to Church. Some schools are interdenominational, others are denominationally affiliated, and others are denominationally controlled schools. But within its structure, whatever it may be, the university must maintain a vital relationship with the Church. There are many concrete ways in which this may be expressed. The university realizes that it is part of the great heritage of the Christian Church and therefore it seeks internally to preserve, explicate, and defend the faith of the Church; and *externally* it does all it can to further the welfare of the Church. The responsibility of the Church is to respect the university as a university. It does this when it respects the academic freedom of the university.

Few problems of the Christian university are so difficult as the problem of academic freedom. By academic freedom we do not mean freedom of speech; this is a political freedom, not an academic freedom. Academic freedom is the freedom to pursue truth according to its own rules, without interference from any source. As soon as the rules for the pursuit of truth are tampered with, then the pursuit is inevitably restricted. A Christian university is a committed institution. It is committed to the thesis that the Christian faith is the truth of God. It states this in a creed or confession which it writes for itself or adopts from its denomination. In a Christian university some tension between academic freedom and Christian commitment would appear to be inevitable. The problem is to find that delicate point of balance where neither scholarship nor conviction is sacrificed. For this situation we suggest the following guide lines:

(i) *The Church must recognize the necessity of scholarship and academic freedom within the university.* Without these there can be no university. Times will occur when a given professor may come under criticism. Both the university and the Church must respect his position and his conclusions. To go contrary — at least provisionally — to the accepted confession requires not only wisdom but also courage. Courage is a great scholarly virtue, and unless the Church and university respect the professor they condone spineless conformity. If it appears that the criticism is wholly justified, then all procedures by the university and the Church must be carried out on the level of highest ethical considerations.

(ii) *The Church must be careful regarding its creed.* Obviously, the more detailed the creed, the more numerous the points of possible conflict and the more trouble with academic freedom.   The creed therefore should be genuinely historical, and in the older sense of the word, ecumenical.   Furthermore, the creed should be carefully worded to state exactly what the Christian Scriptures commit us to in essential matters.   The Church must ask only for general consent given sincerely. When it asks for more than general consent, it places the creed on the level of Scripture; but it has the right to ask that this be made sincerely, for the very integrity of the professor requires this.

(iii) *The professor must not confuse freedom of speech with academic freedom.* Freedom of speech is a political concept and defends the right of a person or persons to private opinions of all sorts.   Academic freedom is the freedom to pursue a subject according to the rules of truth.   But it is not unusual for professors to confuse freedom of speech and freedom in the quest of truth.   The professor is not free to use his lecture desk as the place for sounding forth purely personal opinion.   He is under contract with the Christian university according to its profession both as Christian and as academic institution, and this contract he must honor.

(iv) *The professor must realize that academic freedom is also a set of responsibilities.* The professor is responsible to the student as the student's academic father.   He is the guide of the young mind, not its tormenter.   He never, therefore, becomes an intellectual sadist, shocking students for the abnormal pleasure of shocking them.   The shock treatment that may be employed to free students from prejudice and meaningless tradition is a pedagogical treatment employed with Christian love and Christian dignity.

The professor is responsible to the health of the Church. The Church is an organism and an organization; it can be helped and it can be hindered; it can be strengthened and it can be weakened.   The conscientious professor always uses the lectern responsibly and constructively.

(v) *If the gift to the professor by the Church and the university is academic freedom, the gift of the professor to the*

Church and the university is integrity. If the professor goes beyond the limits of the confession, he ought to say so. He should not be sought out but should make his convictions known to the university administration. Heresy trials are odious and harmful, no matter where the truth or the right lies. Such affairs can be avoided if the integrity of the professor is such that he spontaneously makes his convictions known.

The professor may be right and the school wrong. But the school operates from a committed position. It does not silence the professor but only requests that he find a school in which his opinions do not conflict with the committed position of the Christian university.

SELECT BIBLIOGRAPHY

Altaner, B., *Patrology*. Freiburg: Herder, 1960.

Augustine, *Christian Instruction. The Fathers of the Church*, Vol. 4. New York: Fathers of the Church, Inc., 1947.

————, *Confessions*. New York: Random House, 1948.

Barclay, William, *Educational Ideals in the Ancient World*. Philadelphia: Westminster, 1959.

————, *The Letter to the Hebrews*. Second edition; Philadelphia: Westminster, 1957.

Beard, Charles, *The Reformation in the Sixteenth Century*. Fifth edition; London: Williams and Norgate, 1907.

Bourke, V. J., *St. Augustine's Quest for Wisdom*. Milwaukee: Bruce, 1945.

Brinton, C. C., *The Shaping of the Modern Mind*. New York: The American Library of World Literature, 1954.

Burtt, E. A., *The Metaphysical Foundations of Modern Science*. New York: Harcourt, Brace, 1925.

Butterfield, Herbert, *Christianity and History*. London: Bell, 1949.

Clark, Gordon, *A Christian Philosophy of Education*. Grand Rapids: Eerdmans, 1946.

————, *A Christian View of Men and Things*. Grand Rapids: Eerdmans, 1952.

————, *Thales to Dewey*. Boston: Houghton-Mifflin, 1957.

Cochrane, C. N., *Christianity and Classical Culture*. New York: Oxford, 1944.

Cubberly, E. P., *The History of Education*. New York: Houghton-Mifflin Co., 1948.

Daly, L. J., *The Medieval University, 1200-1400*. London: Sheed and Ward, 1961.

Eadie, Douglas, *Religion on the Campus*. Redlands: University of Redlands, 1961.

Eby, F., *The Development of Modern Education*. New York: Prentice Hall, 1924.

Flexner, Abraham, *Universities, American, German, English*. New York: Oxford, 1930.

Harbison, E. Harris, *The Christian Scholar in the Age of the Reformation*. New York: Scribner, 1957.

Harrold, C. F., *John Henry Newman*. New York: Longmans, Green, 1945.

Haskins, C. H., *The Rise of the Universities*. New York: Cornell, 1957.

Helmreich, E. C., *Religious Education in German Schools*. Cambridge: Harvard, 1959.

Hildebrandt, Franz, *Melanchthon: Alien or Ally?* Cambridge: The University Press, 1946.

Kolfhaus, Wilhelm, Dr. *Abraham Kuyper, 1837-1920, Ein Lebensbericht*. Zweite auflage; F. W. Köhler: Eberfeld, 1924.

Kuyper, Abraham, *Calvinism*. Grand Rapids: Eerdmans, n.d.

———, *Principles of Sacred Theology*. Grand Rapids: Eerdmans, n.d.

———, *The Work of the Holy Spirit*. Grand Rapids: Eerdmans, n.d.

Manschreck, Clyde, *Melanchthon, the Quiet Reformer*. New York: Abingdon Press, 1958.

Moberly, Walter, *The Crisis in the University*. London: S.C.M. Press, 1949.

Newman, John Henry, *The Idea of a University*. New York: Holt, Rinehart and Winston, 1960.

———, *On the Scope and Nature of University Education*. New York: E. P. Dutton, 1933.

Paulsen, F., *The German Universities*. New York: Macmillan, 1895.

Pope, Hugh, *St. Augustine of Hippo*. London: Sands and Co., 1937.

Randall, J. H., Jr., *The Making of the Modern Mind*. Second edition; New York: Houghton-Mifflin, 1940.

Rashdall, Hastings, *Universities of Europe in the Middle Ages*. Three vols.; Oxford: University Press, 1936.

Rusk, R. R., *The Doctrines of the Great Educators*. Revised edition; New York: St. Martin's Press, 1954.

Schwiebert, E. G., *Luther and His Times*. St. Louis: Concordia, 1950.

Sperl, A., *Melanchthon zwischen Humanismus und Reformation*. München: Chr. Kaiser, 1959.

Stupperich, Robert, *Der unbekannte Melanchthon*. Stuttgart: W. Kohlhammer, 1961.

Trueblood, Elton, *The Idea of a College*. New York: Harper, 1959.

Vanden Berg, Frank, *Abraham Kuyper*. Grand Rapids: Eerdmans, 1959.

Zylstra, H., *A Testament of Vision*. Grand Rapids: Eerdmans, 1958.

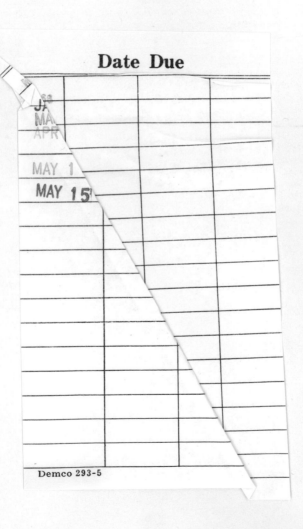